PIANO · VOCAL / PIANO SOLOS

HIT THE KEYS!

CHRISTMAS FAVORITES

COLLECTED SHEET MUSIC: FESTIVE AND FUN

T0058890

Produced by
Alfred Music Publishing Co., Inc.
P.O. Box 10003
Van Nuys, CA 91410-0003
alfred.com

Printed in USA.

ISBN-10: 0-7390-8300-7
ISBN-13: 978-0-7390-8300-0

Cover photo: Christmas Tree - Santa's Sleigh © iStockphoto.com / nokee

Alfred Cares. Contents printed on 100% recycled paper.

CONTENTS

ANGELS WE HAVE HEARD ON HIGH

TRADITIONAL

Chorus:

AULD LANG SYNE

ROBERT BURNS

7

Chorus:

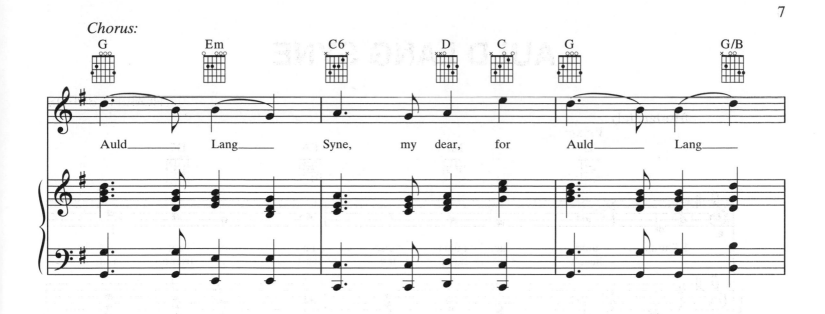

Auld Lang Syne, my dear, for Auld Lang

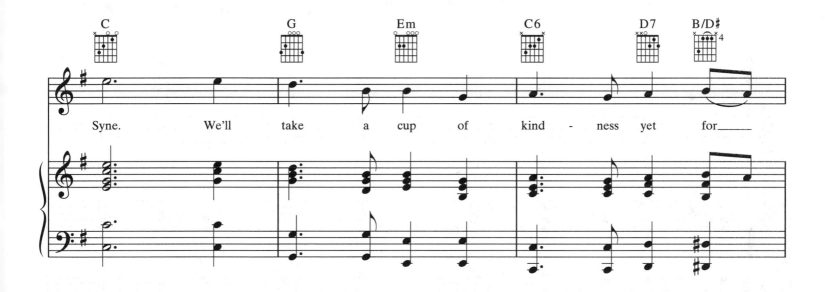

Syne. We'll take a cup of kind - ness yet for

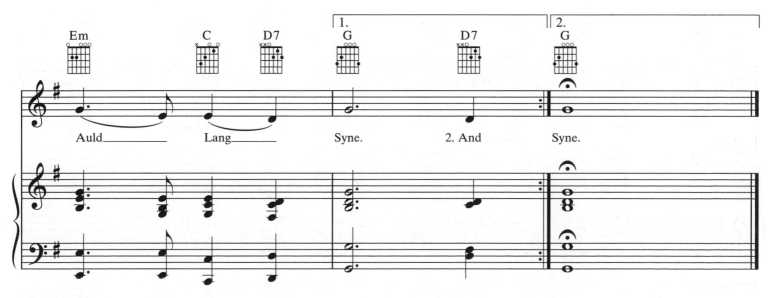

Auld Lang Syne. 2. And Syne.

8

BELIEVE
(from *The Polar Express*)

Words and Music by
ALAN SILVESTRI and GLEN BALLARD

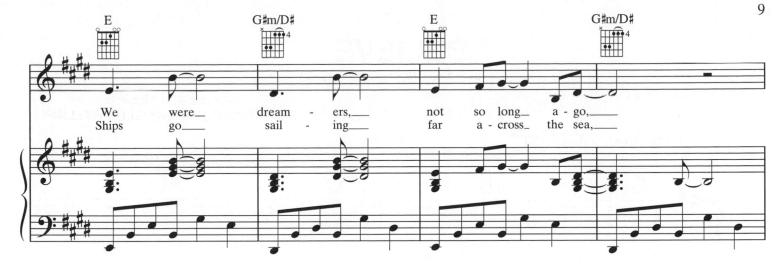

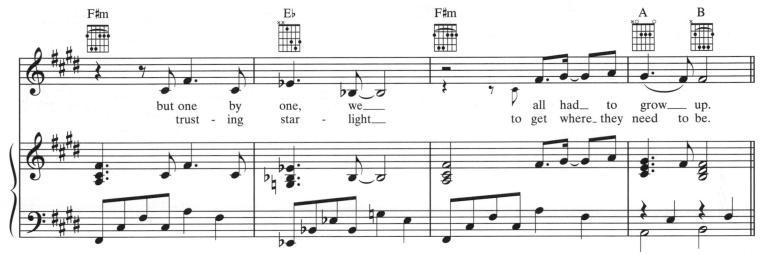

Believe - 4 - 2

9

hear the mel - o - dy___ that's play-ing. There's no time to waste,___ there's so

much to cel - e - brate.___ Be - lieve in what you feel___ in - side___ and

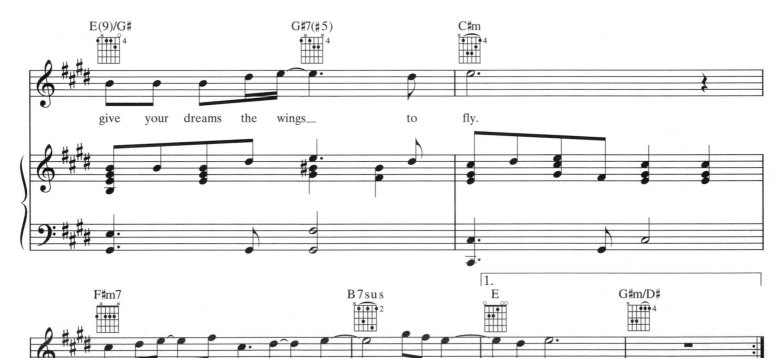

give your dreams the wings___ to fly.

You have ev - 'ry-thing you___ need___ if you just___ be - lieve.

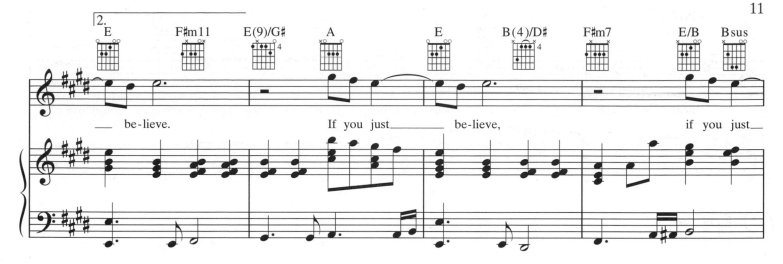

be-lieve. If you just___ be-lieve, if you just___

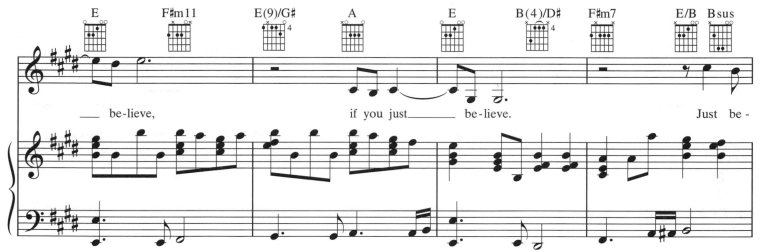

___ be-lieve, if you just___ be-lieve. Just be-

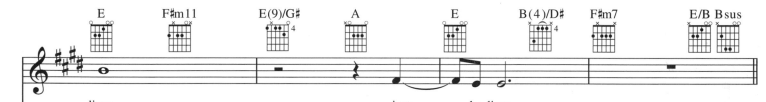

lieve, just___ be-lieve.

Repeat ad lib. and fade

BREATH OF HEAVEN (MARY'S SONG)

Words and Music by
AMY GRANT and CHRIS EATON

Slowly, with expression ♩ = 58

Verse 1:

1. I have trav-eled__ man-y moon-less__ nights,__ cold and wea-ry__ with a

Breath of Heaven (Mary's Song) - 7 - 1

14   *Verse 2:*

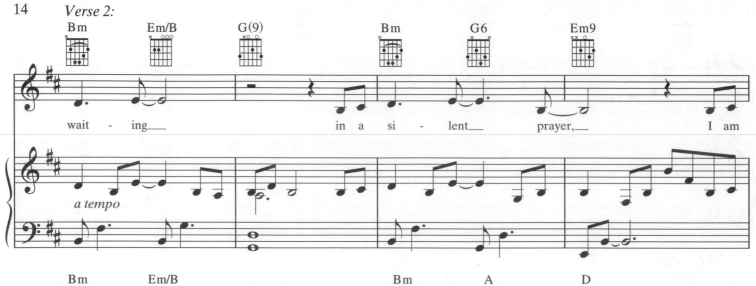

wait - ing____ in a si - lent____ prayer,____ I am

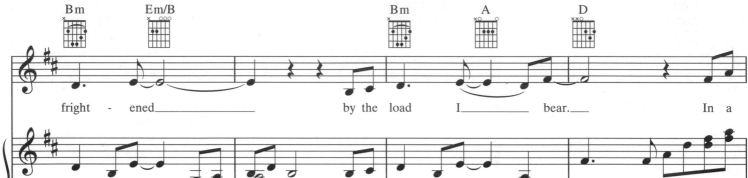

fright - ened_____ by the load I_____ bear.____ In a

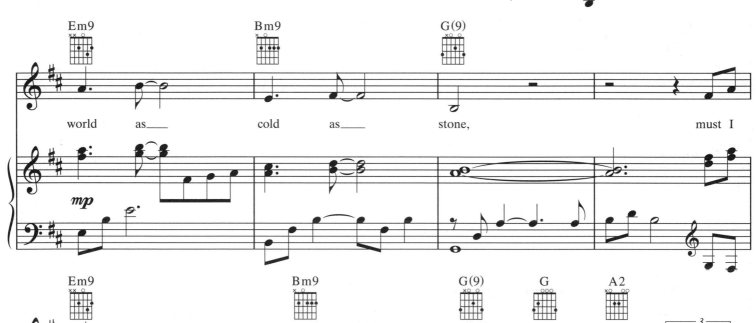

world as____ cold as____ stone, must I

walk this____ path a - lone?____ Be_____ with me

18

Breath of Heaven (Mary's Song) - 7 - 7

CHRISTMAS CANON

Words and Music by
PAUL O'NEILL

Christmas Canon - 5 - 1

20

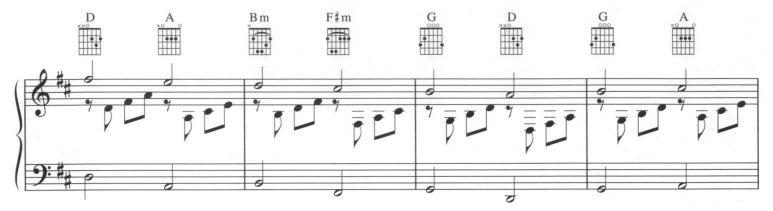

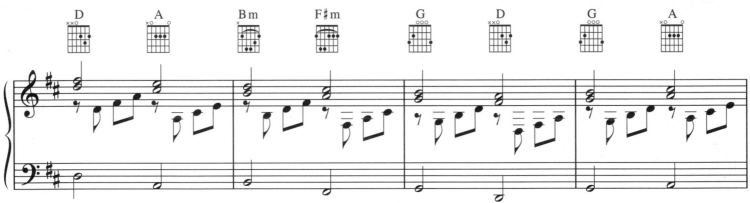

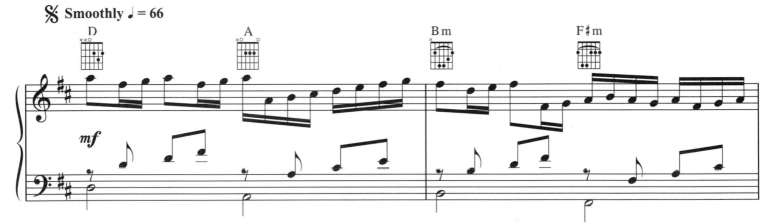

Smoothly ♩ = 66

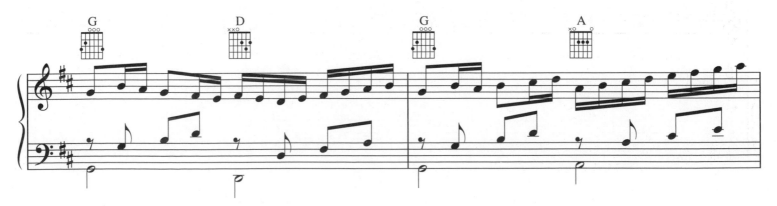

Christmas Canon - 5 - 2

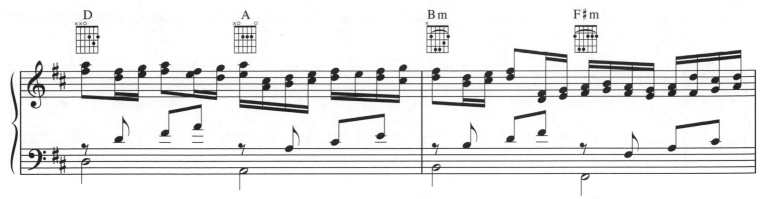

To Coda ✛

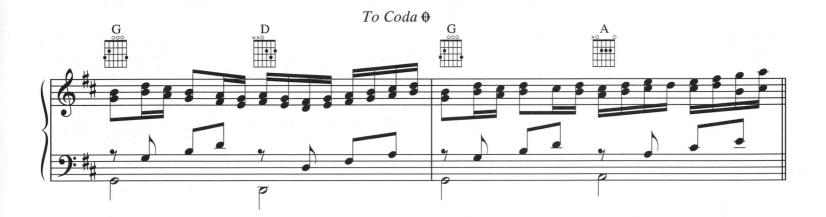

This night we pray our lives will show this dream He had each child still knows.

This night we pray our lives will show this dream He had each child still knows.

Christmas Canon - 5 - 3

CHRISTMAS COMES BUT ONCE A YEAR

Words by
RONALD CADMUS

Music by
MARIO LOMBARDO

Christmas comes but once a year, a sea-son to spread great
Christmas comes but once a year, green wreaths tied with bows of

cheer,
red,

cher-ish-ing time with fam-i-ly,
sil-ver bells ring and rein-deers fly.

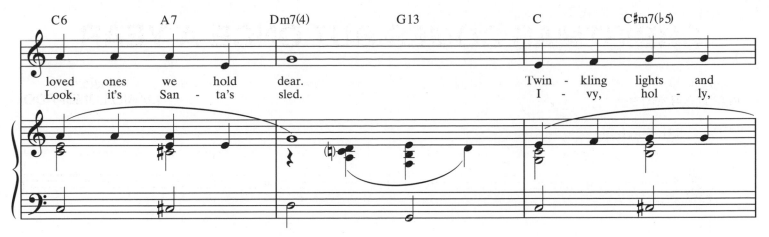

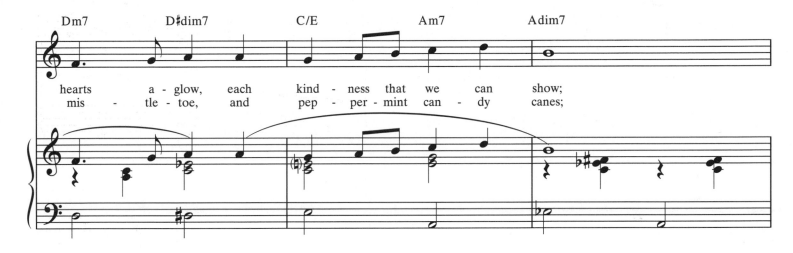

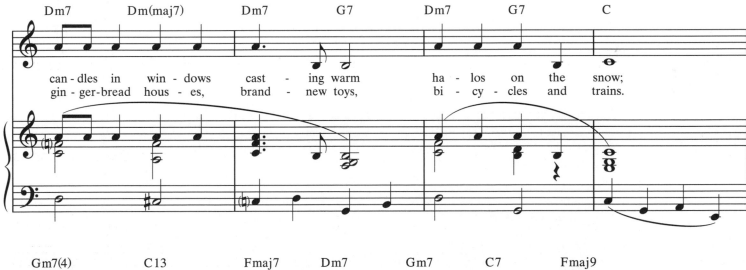

CHRISTMAS EVE / SARAJEVO 12/24

Music by
PAUL O'NEILL and ROBERT KINKEL

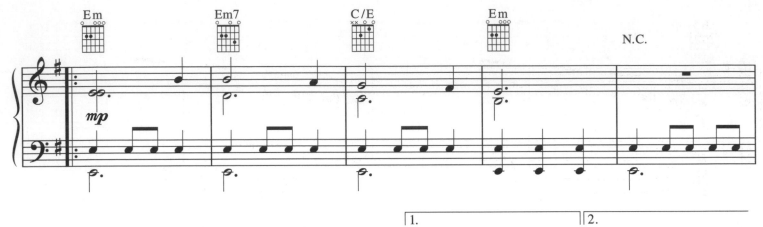

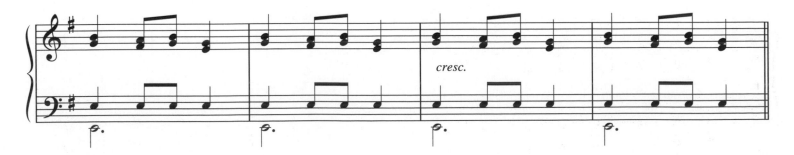

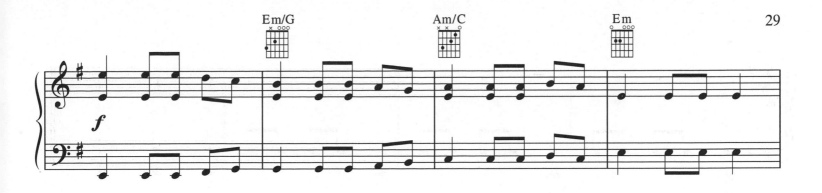

30

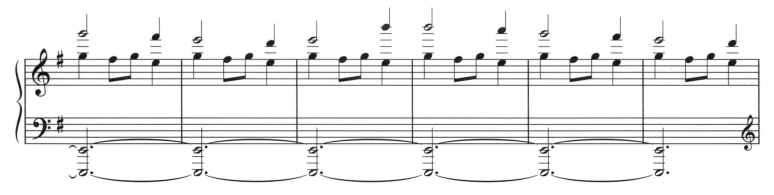

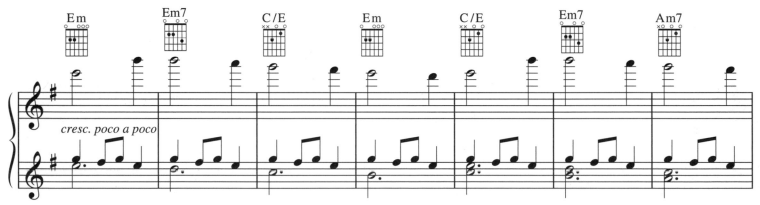

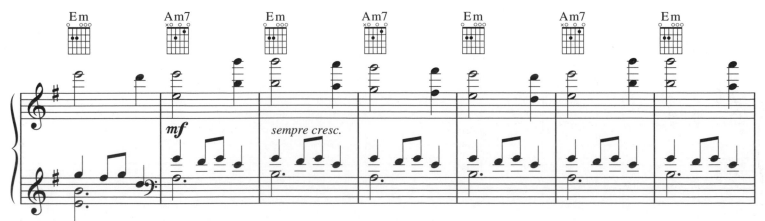

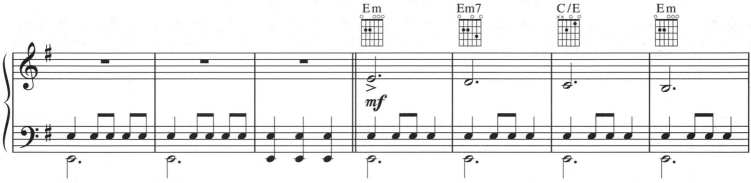

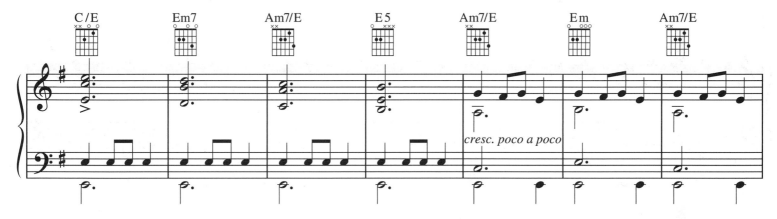

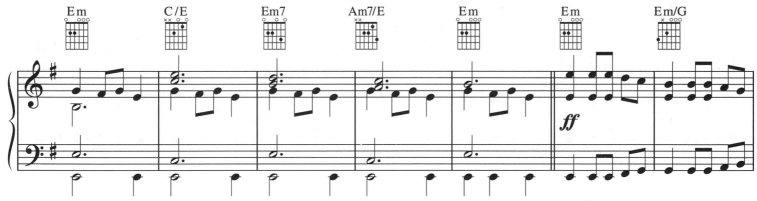

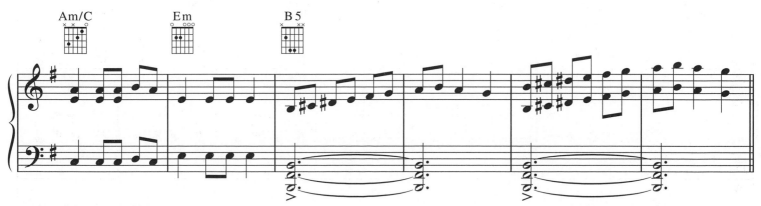

Christmas Eve / Sarajevo 12/24 - 7 - 5

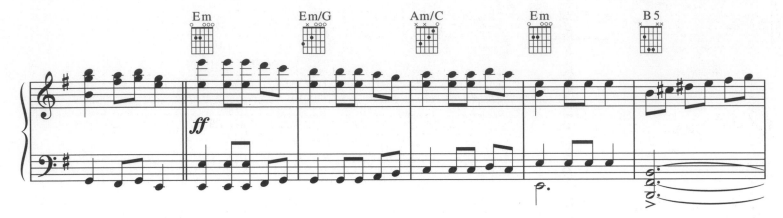

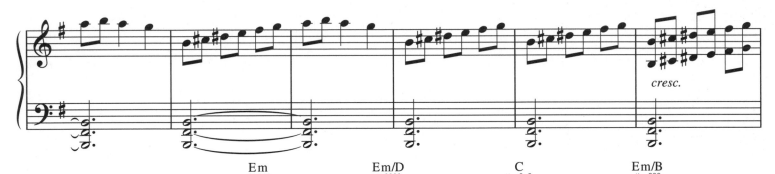

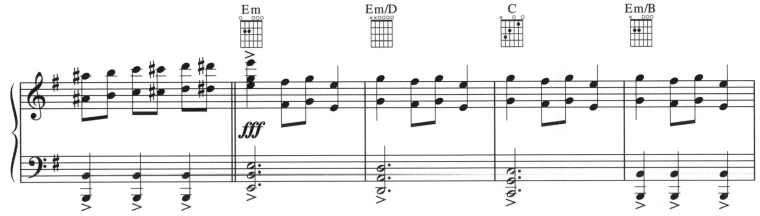

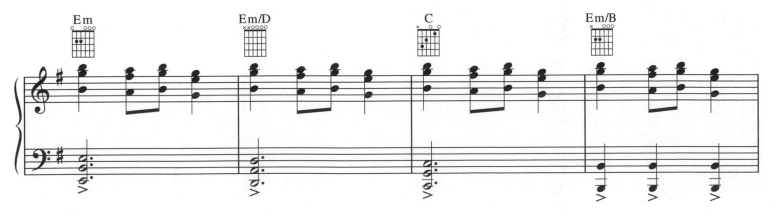

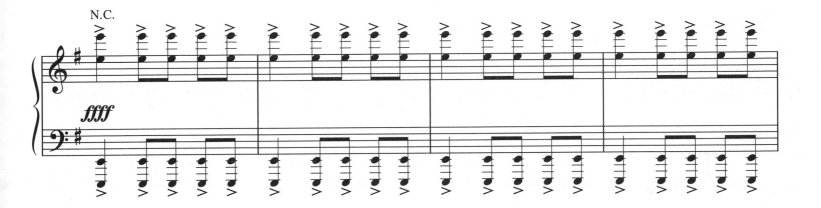

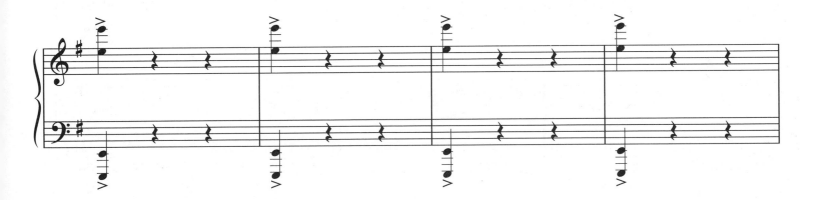

CHRISTMAS WRAPPING

Words and Music by
CHRIS BUTLER

Moderately ♩ = 112

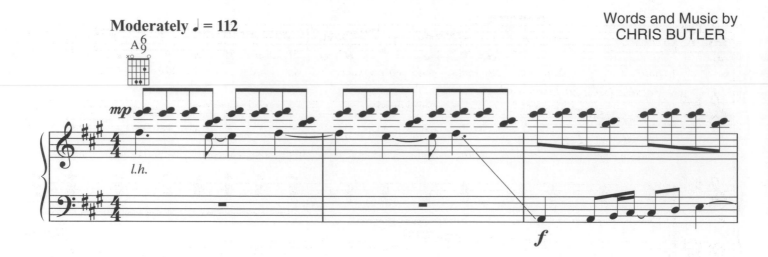

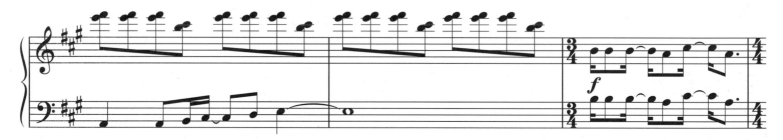

Christmas Wrapping - 10 - 1

Verse 1 (sing 1st time only):

1. *Bah!* *hum-bug!* No, that's too strong 'cause it is my fa-v'rite hol-i-day,___ but

Verse 2 (sing 2nd time only):

2. Cal-en-dar pic-ture, fro-zen land-scape chilled this room for twen-ty-four days.

all this year's been a bus-y blur. Don't think I have the en-er-gy___ to

Ev-er-greens, spar-kling snow, *get this win-ter o-ver with!* Flash-back to

add to my___ al-read-y mad rush just 'cause it's 'tis the sea-son. The

spring-time, saw him a-gain,___ would-'a been good to go___ for lunch,

deck those halls, trim those trees, raise up cups of Christ-mas cheer.

Now the cal-en-dar's just one page, and of course, I am ex-cit-ed. To-

I just need to catch my breath, Christ-mas by my-self this

night's the night, I've set my mind not to do too much a-bout

year.

it.

40

waited all night for him to show,— this time his car would-n't go.— For-

said, "Me, too, but why are you...— you mean you for-got— cran-ber-ries too?"— Then

get it, it's cold, it's get-ting late,— trudge on home to cel-e-brate in a

sud-den-ly— we laughed— and laughed,— caught on to what was hap-pen-ing,— that

qui-et way, un - wind, do-ing Christ-mas right— this

Christ-mas mag-ic's brought this tale to a ver-y hap-py end -

42

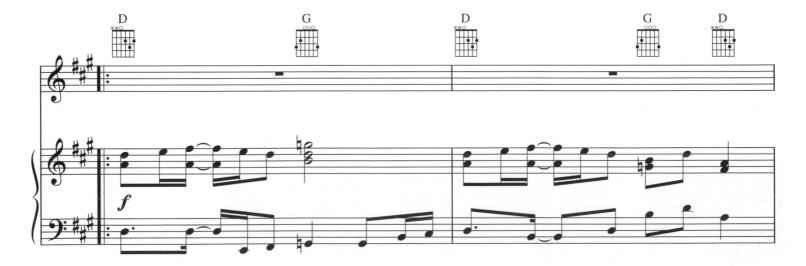

CHRISTMAS IN KILLARNEY

Words and Music by
JOHN REDMOND, JAMES CAVANAUGH
and FRANK WELDON

Christ - mas in Kil - lar - ney is won - der - ful to see.

Lis - ten to my sto - ry and I'll take you back with me. The

hol - ly green, the i - vy green, the pret - ti - est pic - ture you've ev - er seen is

DANCE OF THE SUGAR-PLUM FAIRY

Music by
PETER I. TCHAIKOVSKY

FELÍZ NAVIDAD

Words and Music by
JOSÉ FELICIANO

Moderately ♩ = 144

Verse:

Fe - líz Na - vi - dad.   Fe - líz Na - vi -

dad.   Fe - líz Na - vi - dad.   Pros - pe - ro a -

Felíz Navidad - 4 - 1

FIRST SNOW

Words and Music by
PAUL O'NEILL

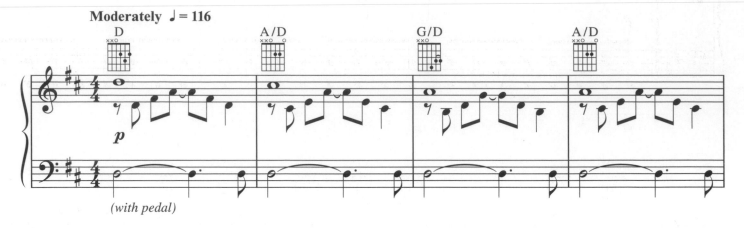

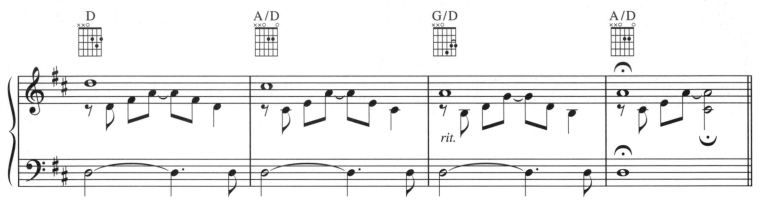

First Snow - 6 - 1

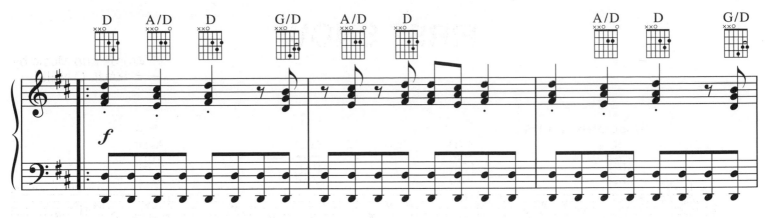

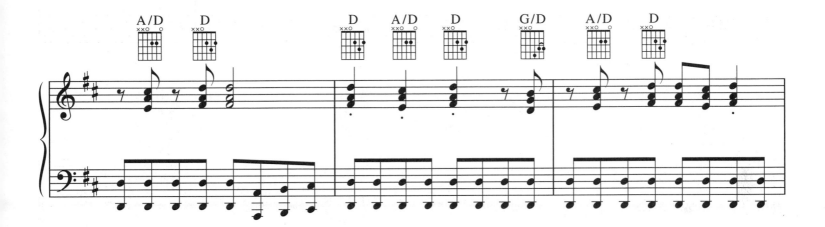

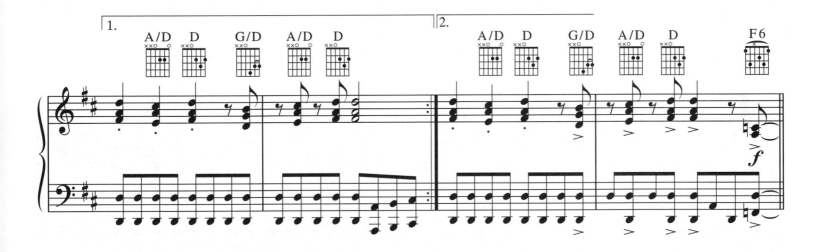

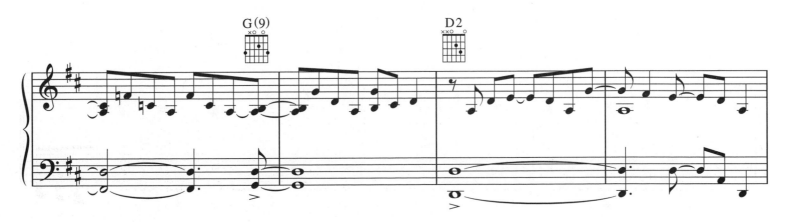

First Snow - 6 - 2

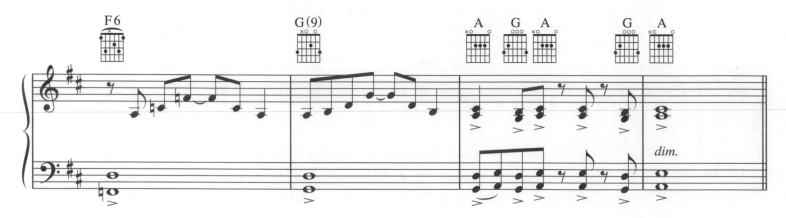

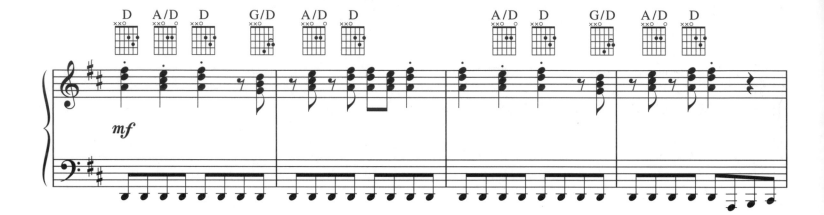

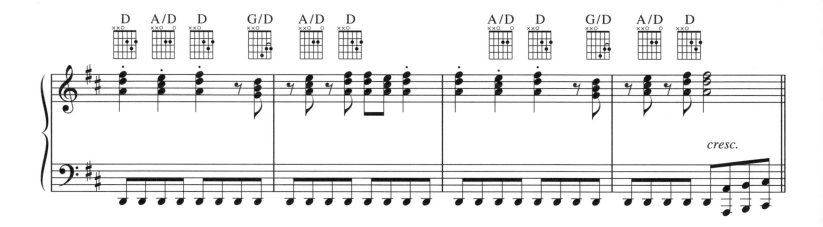

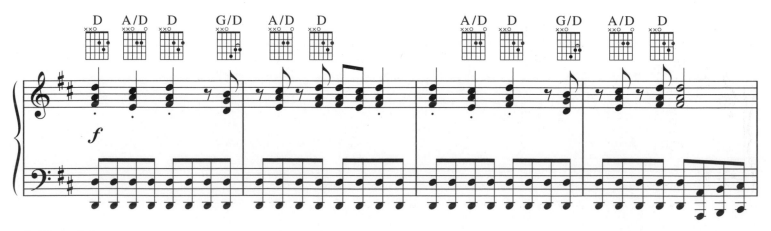

First Snow - 6 - 3

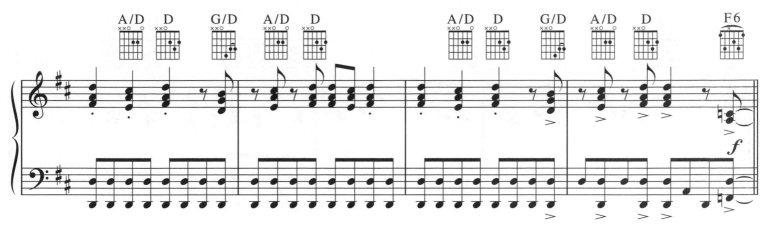

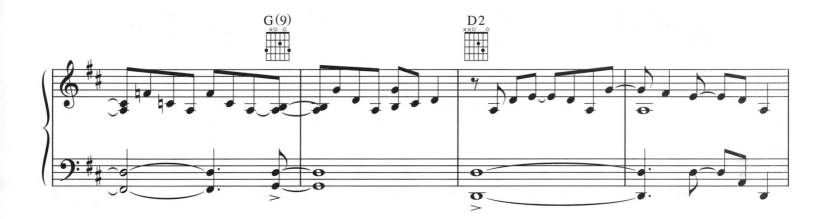

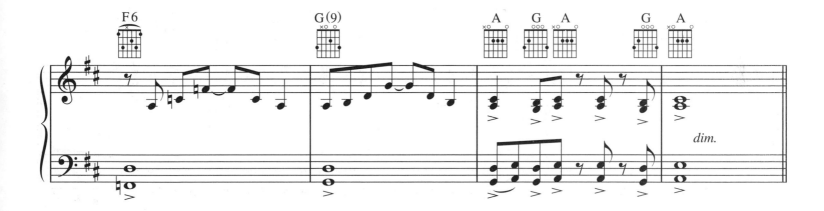

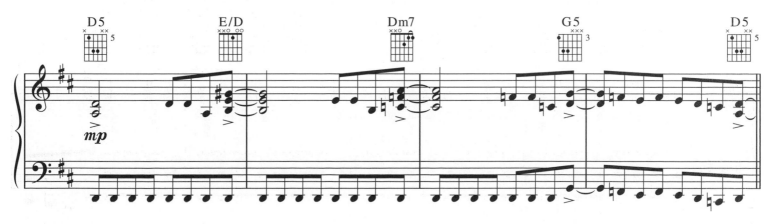

First Snow - 6 - 4

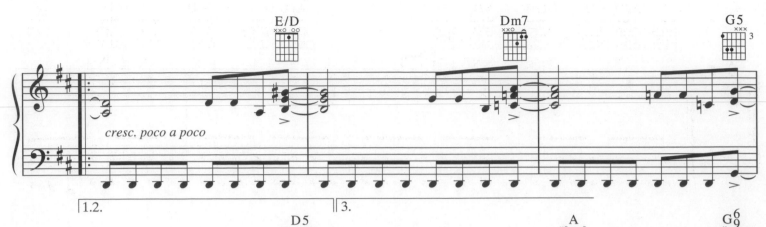

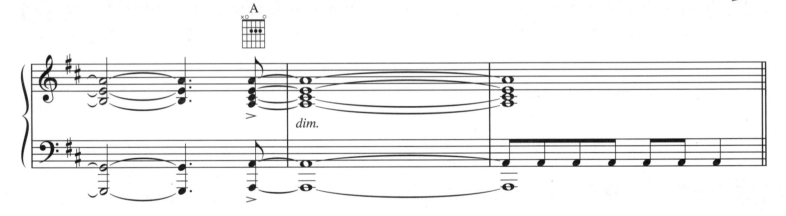

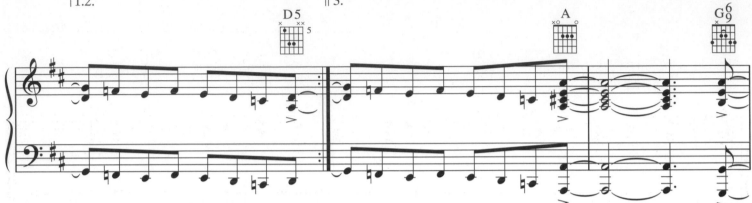

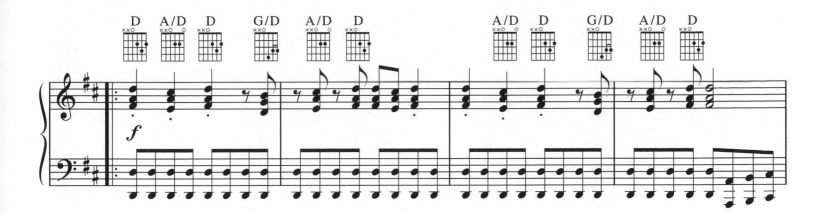

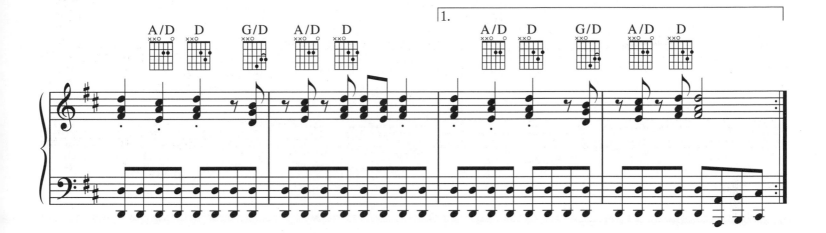

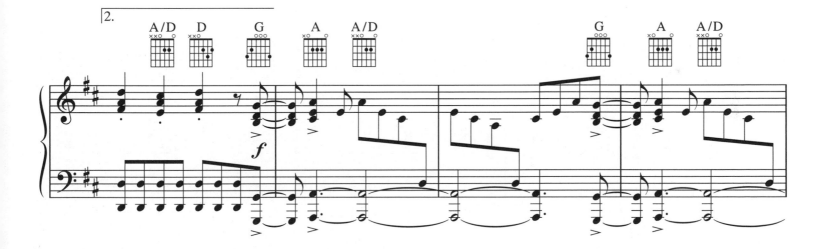

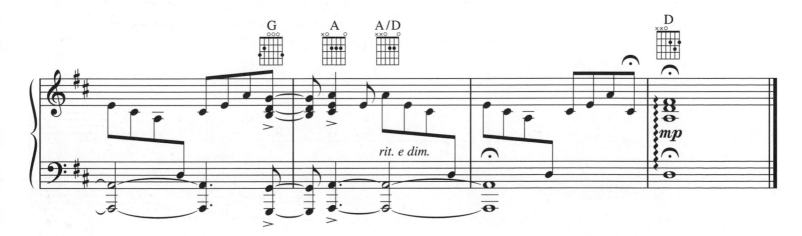

First Snow - 6 - 6

FOR UNTO US A CHILD IS BORN

(from *The Messiah*)

By GEORGE FRIDERIC HANDEL

For Unto Us a Child Is Born - 9 - 1

60

us, a Son is giv-en, Son is giv-en. And the gov-ern-ment shall be up-on His shoul -

der. And the gov-ern-ment shall be up-on His shoul - der. And the gov-ern-ment shall

be up-on His shoul-der, and His Name shall be call-ed

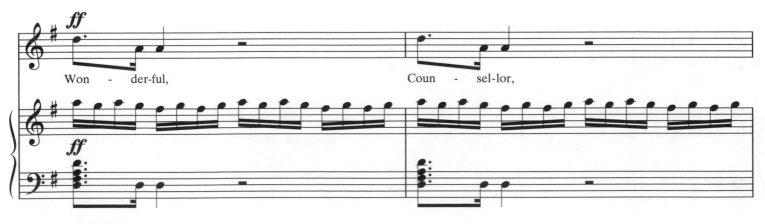

Won - der-ful, Coun - sel-lor,

For Unto Us a Child Is Born - 9 - 3

For Unto Us a Child Is Born - 9 - 4

62

be up-on His shoul - der. And His Name, and His Name shall be call-ed

Won - der-ful, Coun - sel-lor,

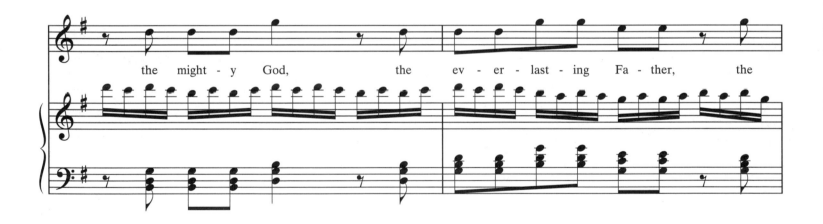

the might - y God, the ev - er - last - ing Fa - ther, the

Prince of Peace. Un - to us a Child is born.__ Un - to us a Child is born.__ Un - to

us a child is born.__ Un-to us a Child is born. Un - to us, a Son is

giv - en. Un - to us, a Son is giv - en. And the gov-ern-ment shall

be up-on His shoul - der. And the gov-ern-ment shall be up-on His shoul -

der. And the gov-ern-ment shall be up-on His shoul-der, and His Name shall be call - ed

For Unto Us a Child Is Born - 9 - 6

64

Won - der-ful, Coun - sel-lor,

the might - y God, the ev - er - last - ing Fa - ther,

Prince of Peace. Un - to us, a Child is born._ Un-to us a Child is born. Un - to

us, a Son is giv - en. Un - to us, a Son is

For Unto Us a Child Is Born - 9 - 7

giv-en. Un-to us,   a Son is giv-en. And the gov-ern-ment, the gov-ern-ment shall

be up-on His shoul-der. And the gov-ern-ment, the gov-ern-ment shall

be up-on His shoul-der, and His Name shall be call-ed.

ff Won-der-ful,   Coun-sel-lor,

66

the might - y God, the ev - er - last - ing Fa - ther, the

Prince of Peace, the ev - er - last - ing Fa - ther, the Prince of Peace.

FROSTY THE SNOWMAN

Words and Music by
STEVE NELSON and JACK ROLLINS

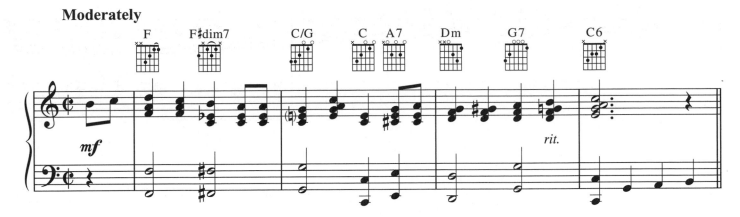

1. Frost - y the snow-man was a jol - ly hap - py soul,___ with a
2. Frost - y the snow-man knew the sun was hot that day,___ so he

corn - cob pipe and a but - ton nose___ and two eyes made out of coal.
said, "Let's run and we'll have some fun___ now be - fore I melt a - way."

Frosty the Snowman - 3 - 1

THE GIFT

Words and Music by
JIM BRICKMAN and
TOM DOUGLAS

The Gift - 5 - 1

Chorus:

gift.

Verse 2:

2. Watch-ing as you soft-ly__ sleep. What I'd give if I__ could__ keep just this mo-ment. If

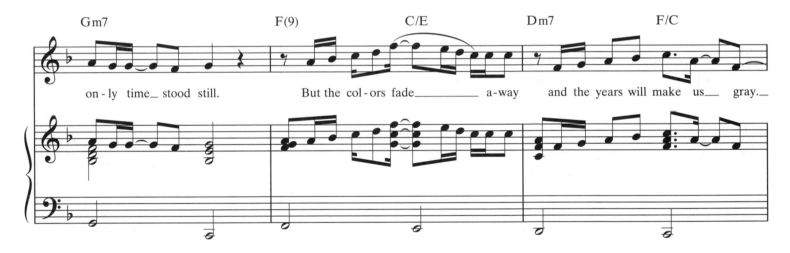

on-ly time_ stood still. But the col-ors fade_____ a-way and the years will make us__ gray.__

__ But, ba-by, in my eyes,__ you'll still be beau-ti-ful._____ And all I want_

The Gift - 5 - 3

%S *Chorus:*

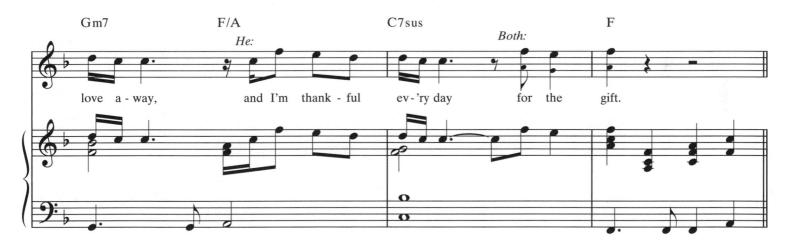

The Gift - 5 - 4

74

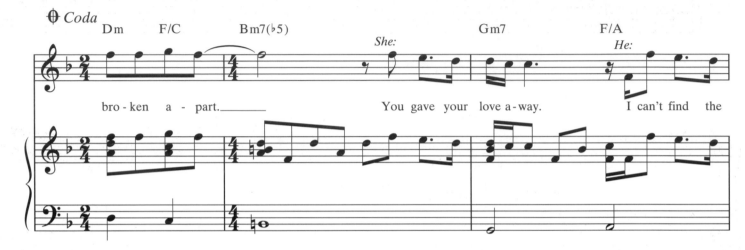

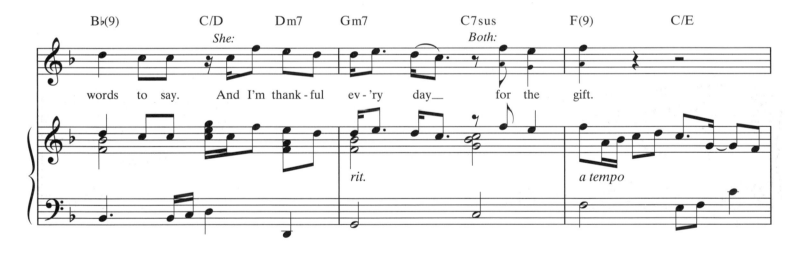

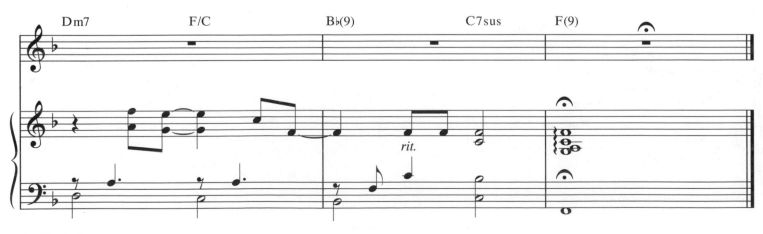

The Gift - 5 - 5

GREENSLEEVES/CAROL OF THE BELLS
(Medley)

TRADITIONAL
Arrangement by JIM BRICKMAN

Moderately slow ♩ = 72

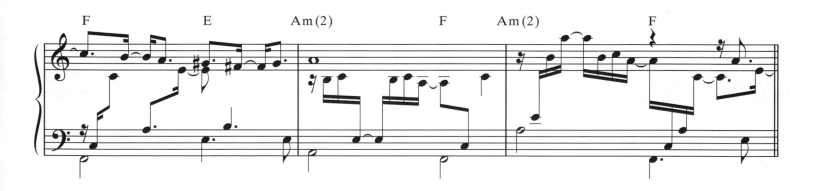

Greensleeves/Carol of the Bells - 5 - 1

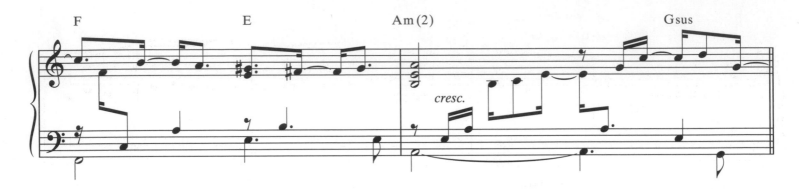

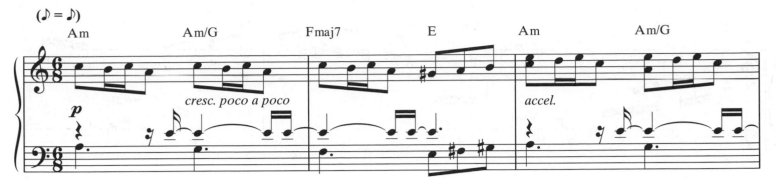

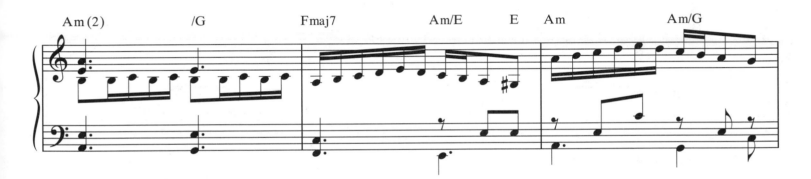

Greensleeves/Carol of the Bells - 5 - 3

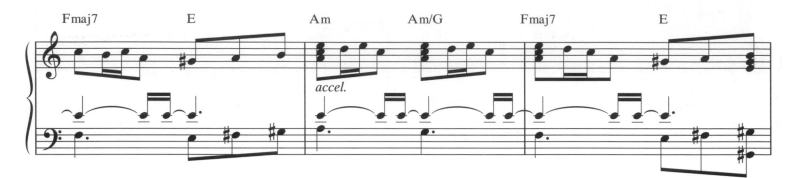

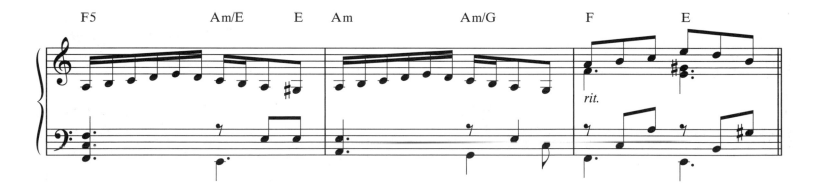

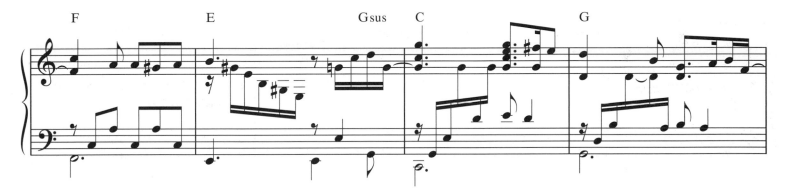

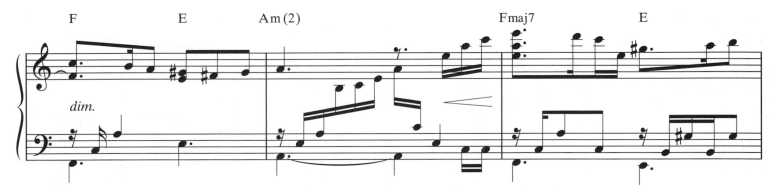

Quickly - tempo ad lib.

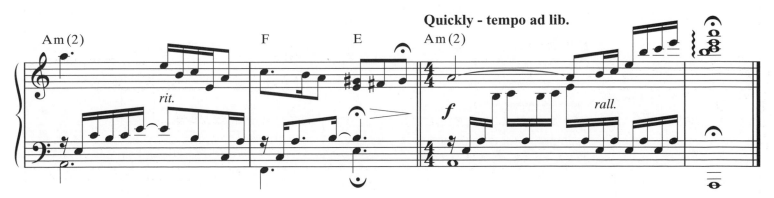

HALLELUJAH! CHORUS

(from *The Messiah*)

By GEORGE FRIDERIC HANDEL

Allegro moderato (♩ = 88)

Hal - le - lu - jah! Hal - le - lu - jah! Hal-le - lu - jah! Hal-le - lu - jah! Hal -

le - lu - jah! Hal - le - lu - jah! Hal - le - lu - jah! Hal-le -

Hallelujah! Chorus - 8 - 1

lu - jah! Hal -le -lu - jah! Hal - le - lu - jah! For the Lord

God om - ni - po - tent reign - eth. Hal-le - lu - jah! Hal-le-lu - jah! Hal-le -

lu - jah! Hal-le-lu - jah! For the Lord God om - ni - po - tent

reign - eth. Hal-le-lu - jah! Hal-le-lu - jah! Hal-le - lu - jah! Hal-le - lu - jah!

Hallelujah! Chorus - 8 - 2

For the Lord God om-ni-po-tent reign---eth.

For the Lord God om-ni-po-tent reign---eth. Hal-le-lu-jah!

Hal-le-lu-jah! Hal-le-lu-jah! For the Lord God om-ni-po-tent

reign---eth Hal - le - lu-jah! The

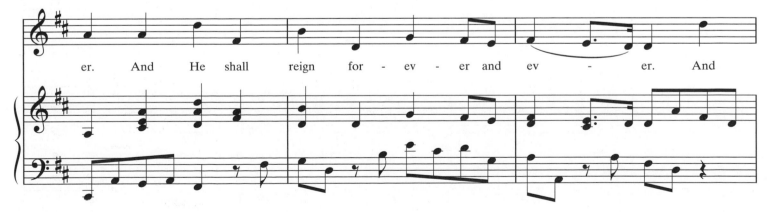

84

He shall reign for - ev - er and ev - er. King of

Kings, for - ev - er and ev - er. Hal - le - lu - jah! Hal - le - lu - jah! and Lord of

Lords. For - ev - er and ev - er. Hal - le - lu - jah! Hal - le - lu - jah! King of

Kings. For - ev - er and ev - er. Hal - le - lu - jah! Hal - le - lu - jah! And Lord of

Hallelujah! Chorus - 8 - 5

Hallelujah! Chorus - 8 - 6

ev - er and ev - er. King of Kings, for - ev - er and

ev - er, and Lord of Lords. Hal-le-lu-jah! Hal-le-lu-jah! And He shall

reign for - ev - er, for - ev - er and ev - er. King of

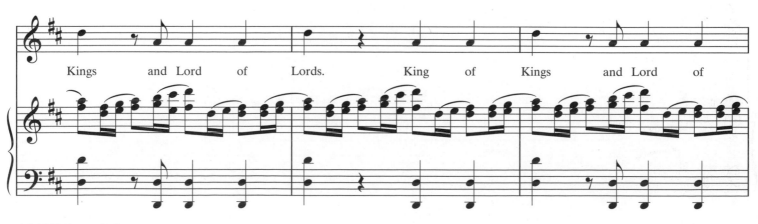

Kings and Lord of Lords. King of Kings and Lord of

Lords. And He shall reign for -

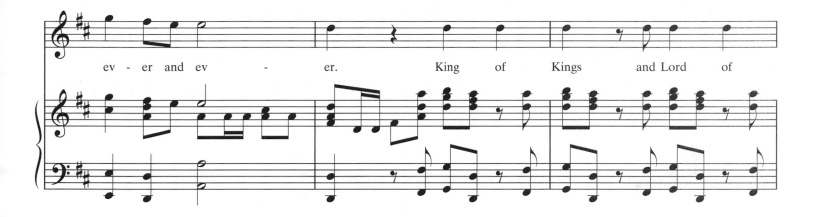

ev - er and ev - er. King of Kings and Lord of

Lords. Hal - le - lu - jah! Hal - le - lu - jah! Hal - le - lu - jah! Hal - le -

Largo
ff

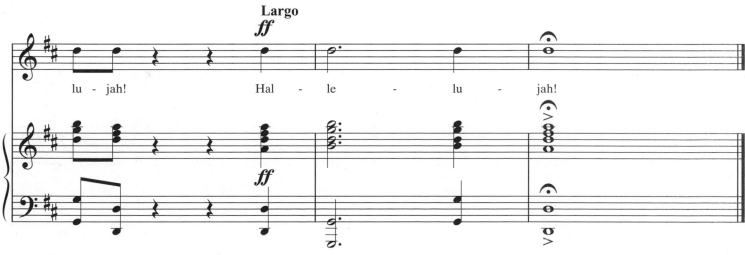

lu - jah! Hal - le - lu - jah!

HAVE YOURSELF A MERRY LITTLE CHRISTMAS

Words and Music by
HUGH MARTIN and RALPH BLANE

Slowly

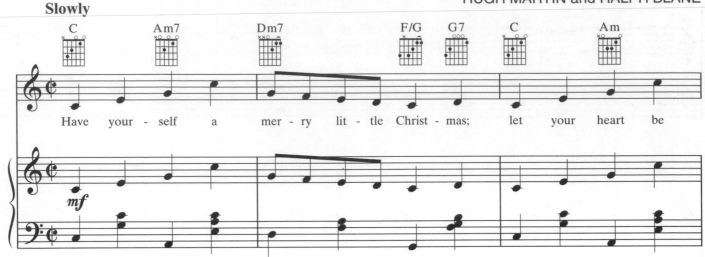

Have your-self a mer-ry lit-tle Christ-mas; let your heart be

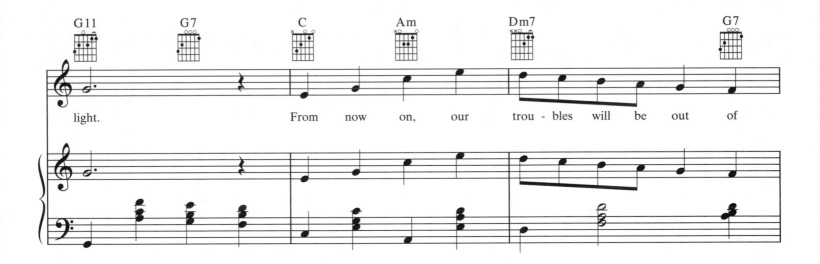

light. From now on, our trou-bles will be out of

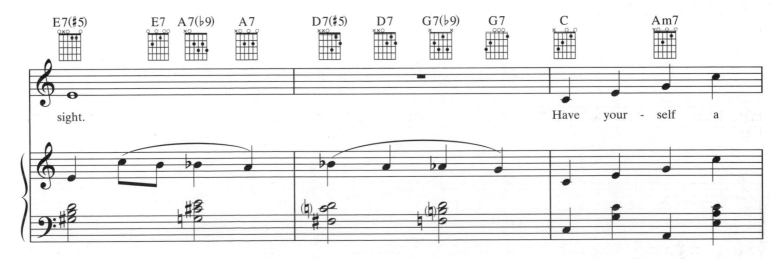

sight. Have your-self a

A HOLLY JOLLY CHRISTMAS

Words and Music by
JOHNNY MARKS

A Holly Jolly Christmas - 3 - 1

93

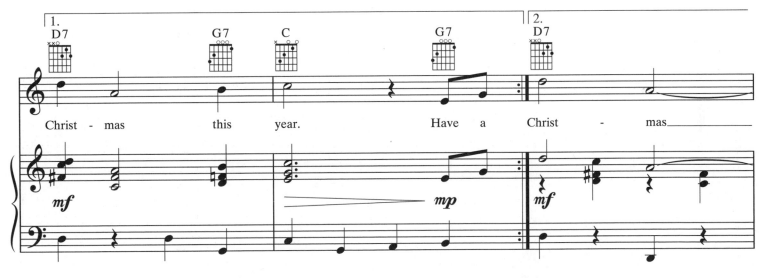

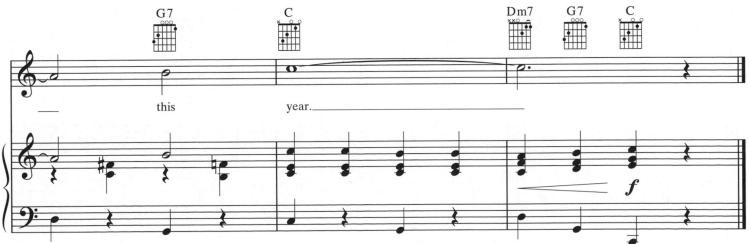

A Holly Jolly Christmas - 3 - 3

HEAT MISER

(from *The Year Without a Santa Claus*)

Words and Music by
JULES BASS and MAURY LAWS

Ragtime feel, with a light shuffle ♩ = 80

Refrain:

I'm Mis - ter Green Christ - mas. I'm Mis - ter Sun.

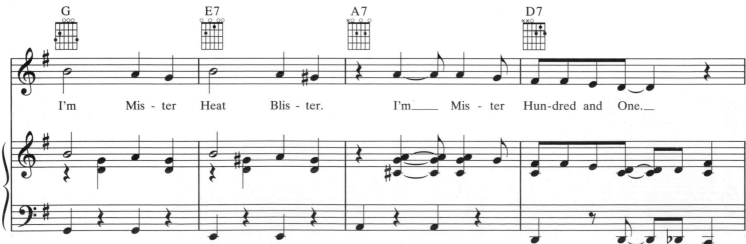

I'm Mis - ter Heat Blis - ter. I'm___ Mis - ter Hun-dred and One.___

Heat Miser - 4 - 1

A7

D7

rath - er have it eight - y, nine - ty, one hun - dred de - grees!

G

(Spoken:) Oh, some like it hot, but I like it REALLY hot! Hee hee!

3 3 3 3 3 3 3 3

D.S. 𝄋 al Coda

3 3 3 3 3 3

Coda

D7 G Ab7 G7

I'm too much. Too much!

𝆑

HOLY, HOLY, HOLY

Traditional
Arranged by JIM BRICKMAN

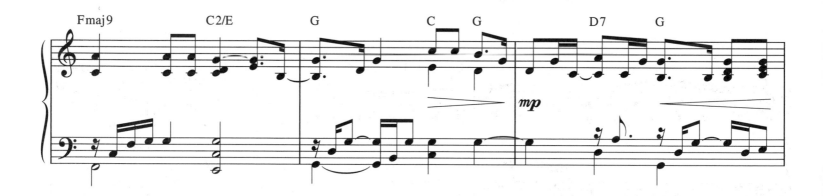

Holy, Holy, Holy - 4 - 1

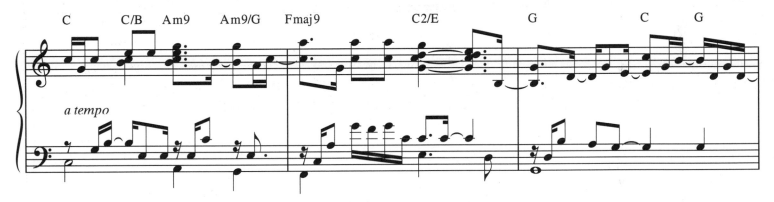

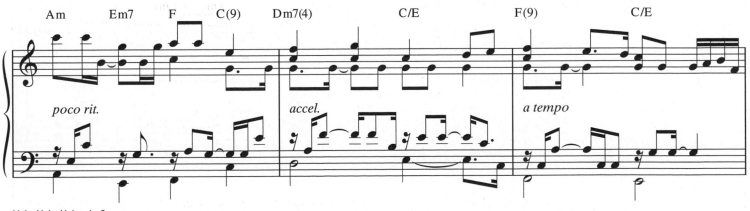

Holy, Holy, Holy - 4 - 2

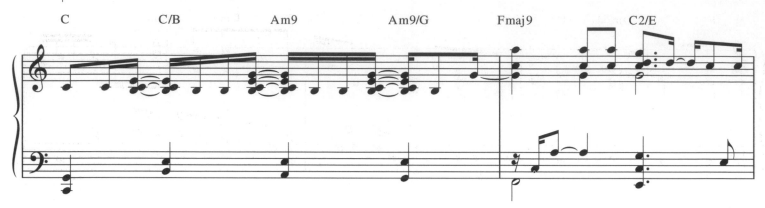

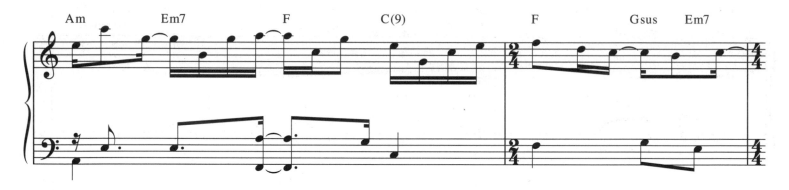

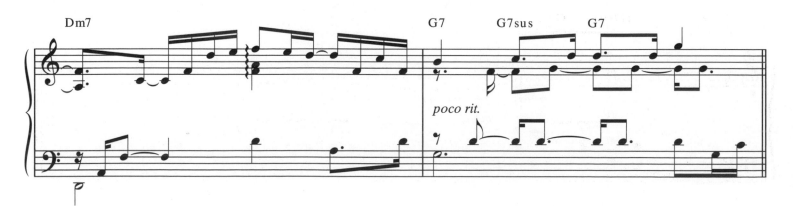

Holy, Holy, Holy - 4 - 3

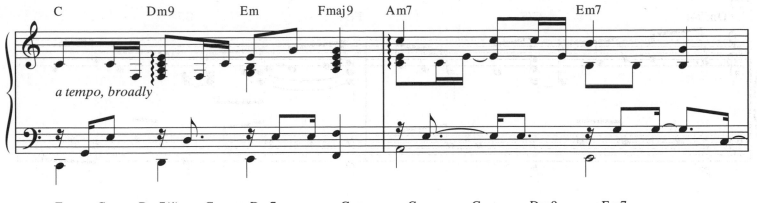

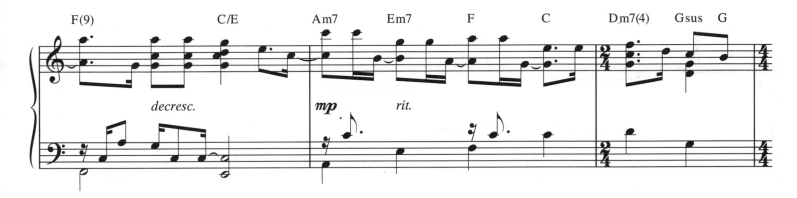

I'LL BE HOME FOR CHRISTMAS

Words by
KIM GANNON

Music by
WALTER KENT

Refrain:

In Memory of Adele Lombardo

IT'S NOT CHRISTMAS WITHOUT YOU

Words and Music by
MARIO LOMBARDO
and JOSEPH LaZIZZA

Moderately, with expression

106

It's Not Christmas Without You - 3 - 2

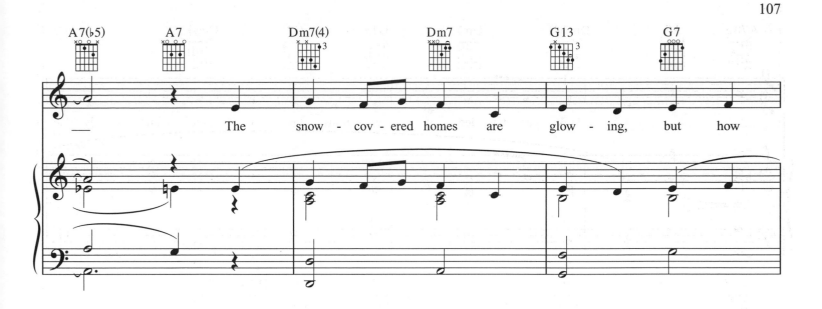

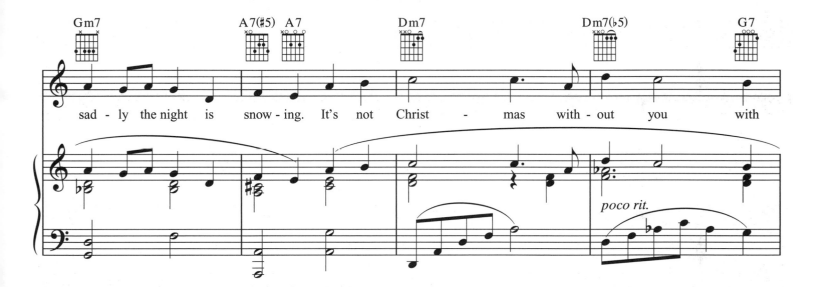

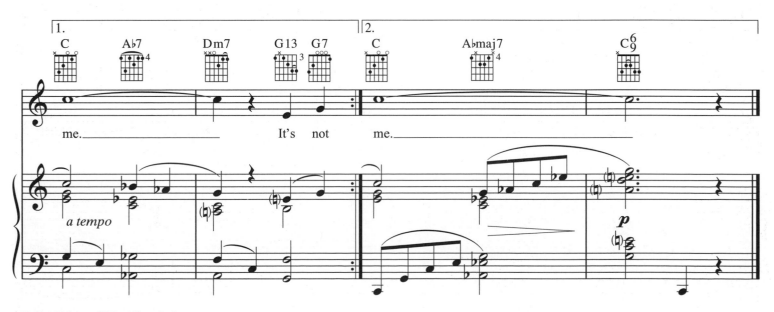

It's Not Christmas Without You - 3 - 3

JESU, JOY OF MAN'S DESIRING

JOHANN SEBASTIAN BACH

Jesu, Joy of Man's Desiring - 4 - 1

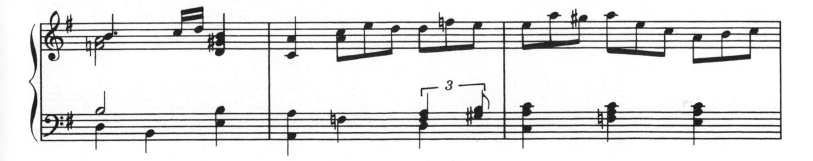

IT'S THE MOST WONDERFUL
TIME OF THE YEAR

Words and Music by
EDDIE POLA and GEORGE WYLE

Bright waltz tempo (Happily)

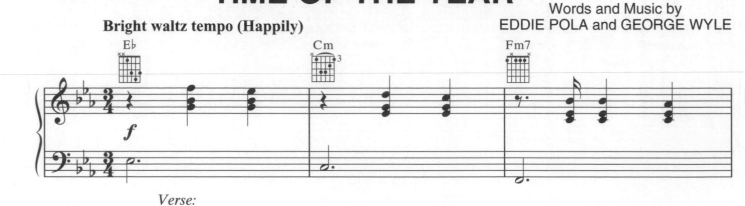

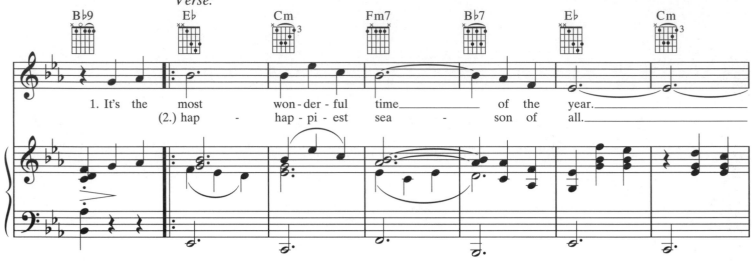

Verse:

1. It's the most won-der-ful time of the year.
(2.) hap - hap-pi-est sea - son of all.

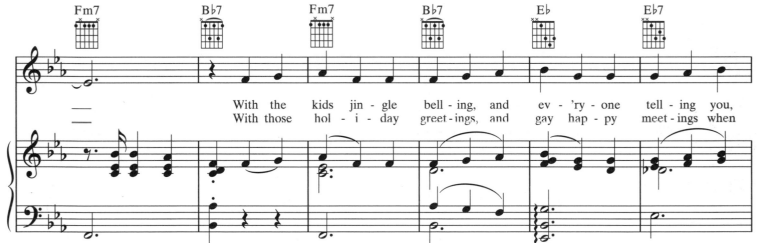

With the kids jin-gle bell-ing, and ev-'ry-one tell-ing you,
With those hol-i-day greet-ings, and gay hap-py meet-ings when

"Be of good cheer," it's the most won-der-ful
friends come to call, it's the hap - hap-pi-est

It's the Most Wonderful Time of the Year - 3 - 1

114

It's the Most Wonderful Time of the Year - 3 - 3

LET IT SNOW! LET IT SNOW! LET IT SNOW!

Words by
SAMMY CAHN

Music by
JULE STYNE

you real - ly hold me tight, all the way home I'll be

warm. The fi - re is slow - ly dy - ing, and, my

dear, we're still good - bye - ing. But as long as you love me

so, let it snow, let it snow, let it snow! Oh, the snow!

Let it Snow! Let it Snow! Let it Snow! - 3 - 3

LAST CHRISTMAS

Words and Music by
GEORGE MICHAEL

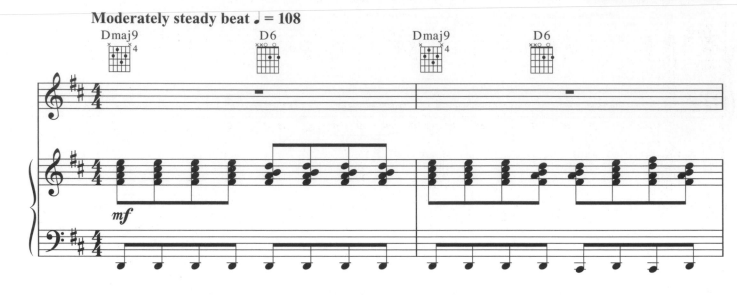

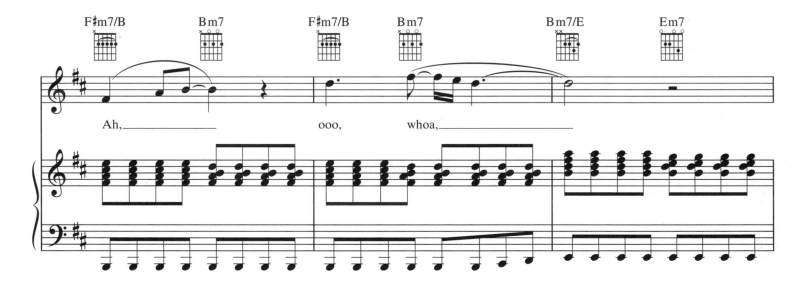

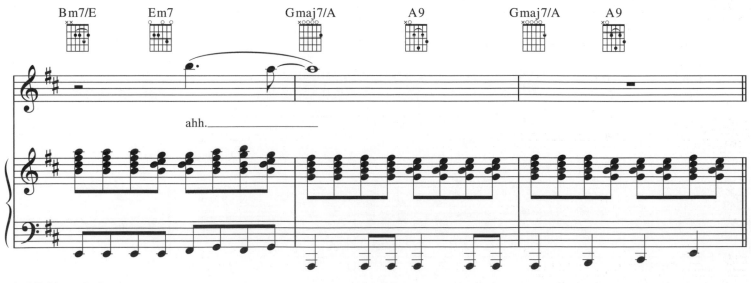

Last Christmas - 6 - 1

120

Verse 1 (sing 1st time only):

1. Once bit - ten and twice shy,_____ I keep my dis - tance but

Verse 2 (sing 2nd time only):

2. A crowd - ed room, friends with tired_ eyes,_____ I'm hid - ing from you

tears still catch_ my eye.____ Tell me, ba - by, do you rec - og - nize_ me?

and your soul_ of ice.____ My god, I thought you were some-one to re - ly___ on.

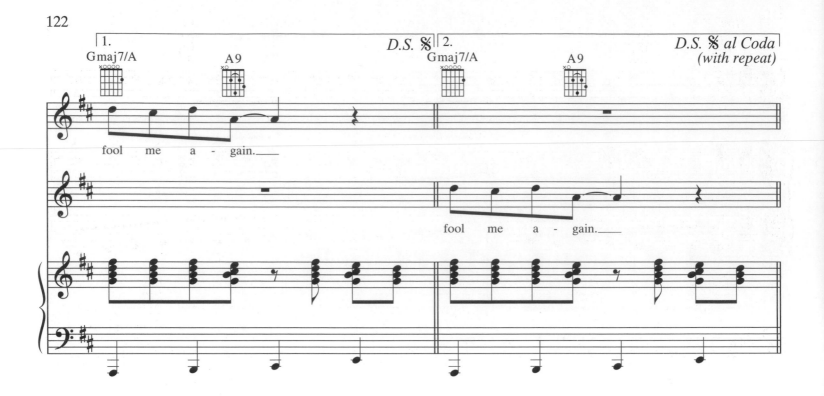

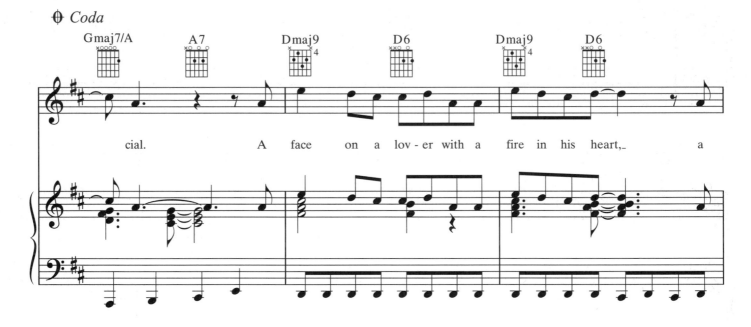

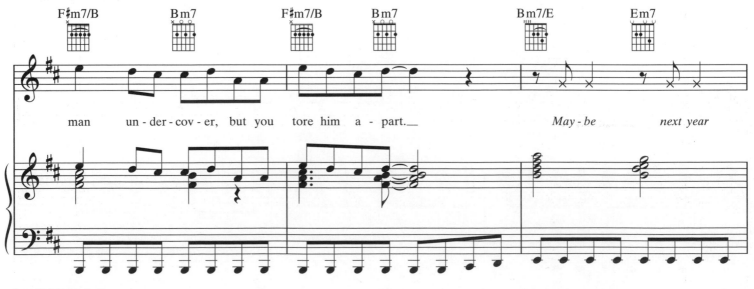

THE LITTLE DRUMMER BOY

Words and Music by
HARRY SIMEONE, HENRY ONORATI
and KATHERINE DAVIS

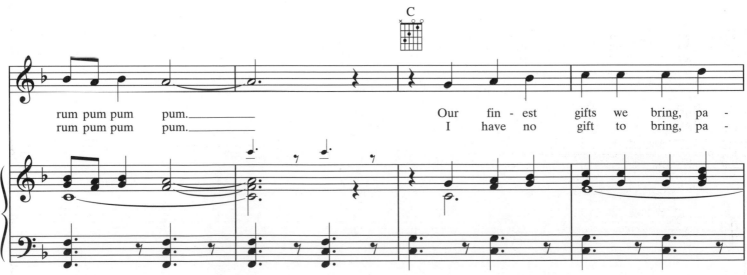

The Little Drummer Boy - 4 - 2

on ___ my drum?___

3. Mar - y nod - ded, pa - rum pum pum pum,___

the ox and lamb kept time, pa - rum pum pum pum.___

I played my drum for Him, pa - rum pum pum pum,___

The Little Drummer Boy - 4 - 4

THE LITTLE DRUMMER BOY / PEACE ON EARTH

PEACE ON EARTH:
Words by
ALAN KOHAN
Music by
LARRY GROSSMAN
and IAN FRASER

THE LITTLE DRUMMER BOY:
Words and Music by
HARRY SIMEONE, HENRY ONORATI
and KATHERINE DAVIS

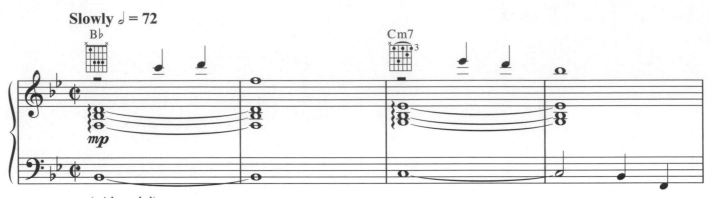

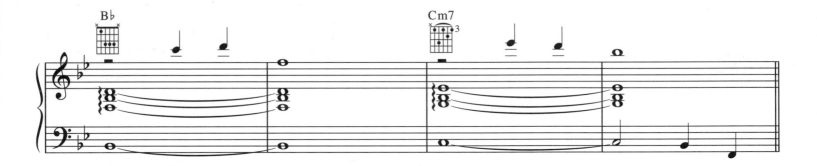

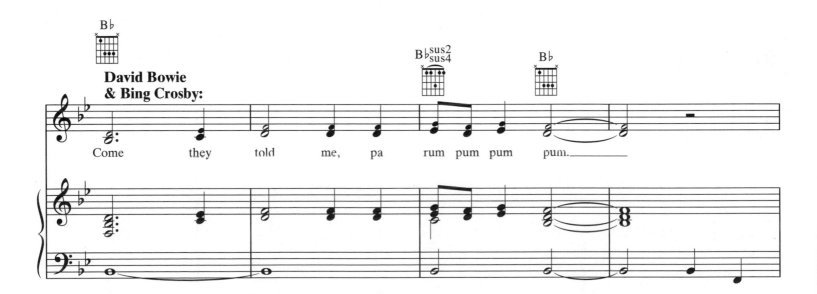

The Little Drummer Boy / Peace on Earth - 5 - 1

132

A MAD RUSSIAN'S CHRISTMAS

Music by
PAUL O'NEILL, ROBERT KINKEL
and PETER ILYICH TCHAIKOVSKY

Slowly ♩ = 50

(with pedal)

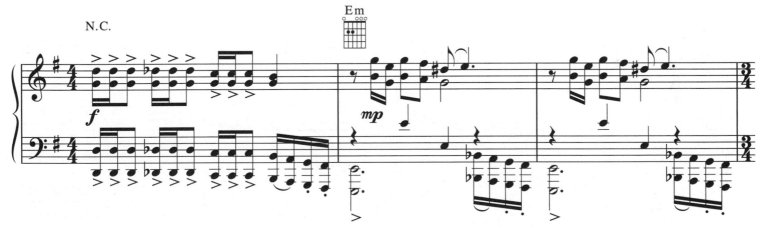

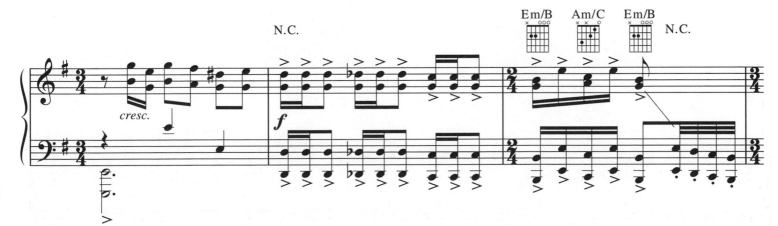

A Mad Russian's Christmas - 9 - 1

134

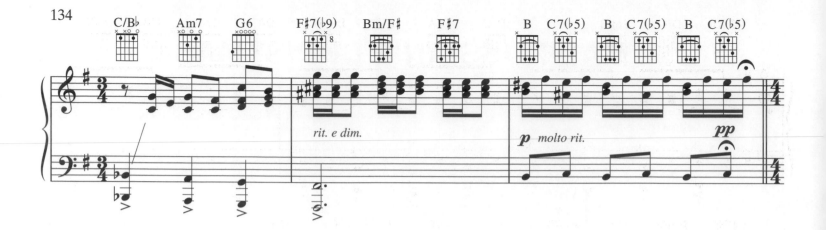

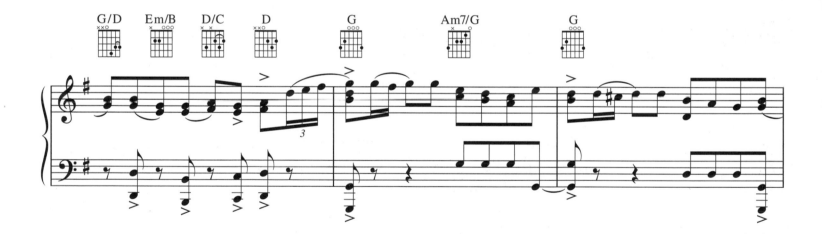

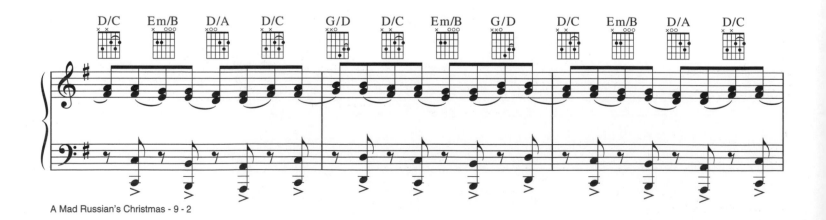

A Mad Russian's Christmas - 9 - 2

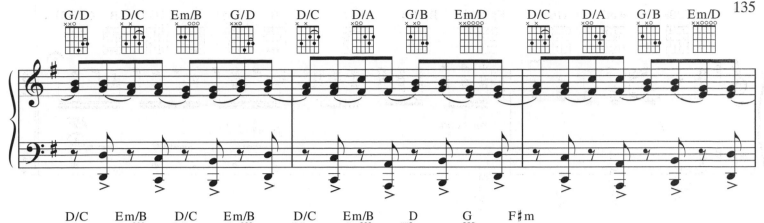
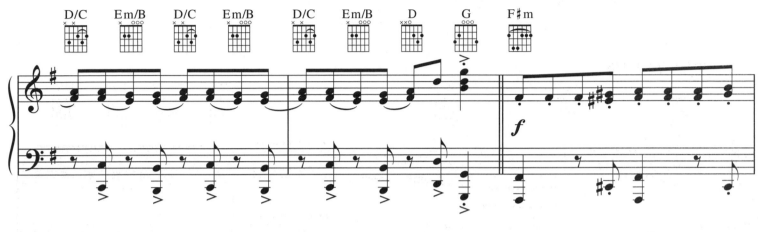

A Mad Russian's Christmas - 9 - 3

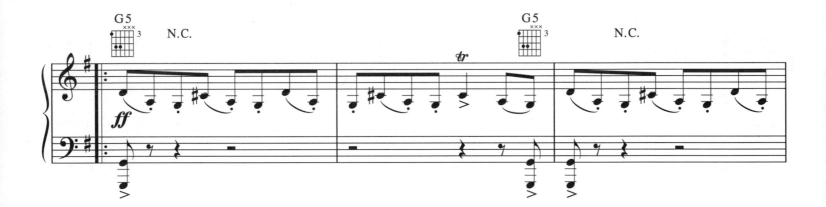

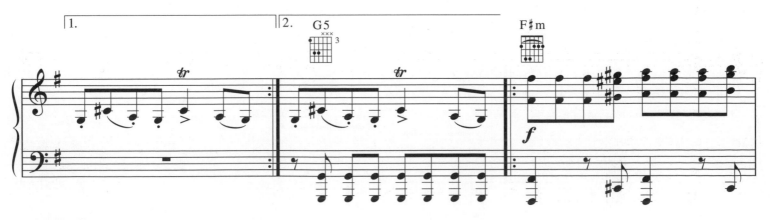

1.2.3.   4.

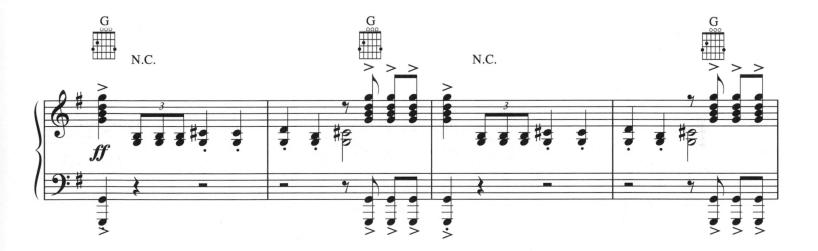

A Mad Russian's Christmas - 9 - 5

138

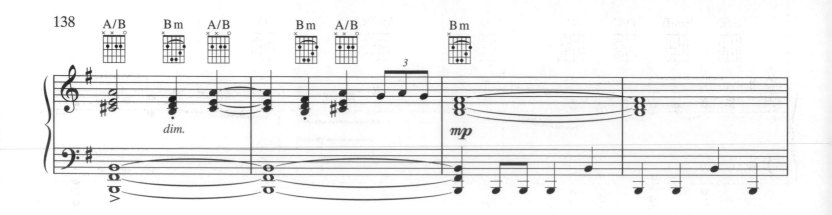

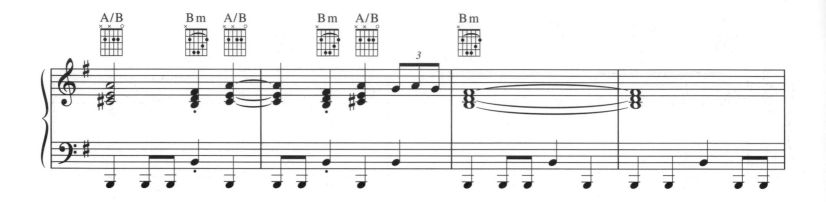

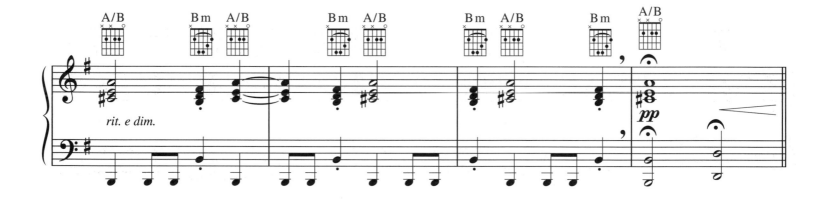

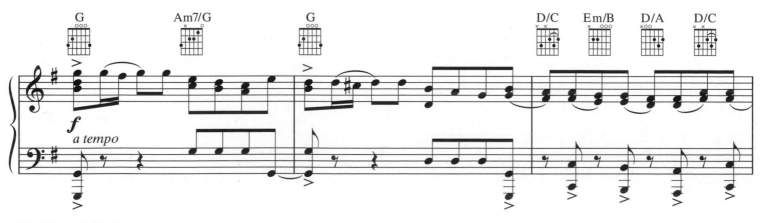

A Mad Russian's Christmas - 9 - 6

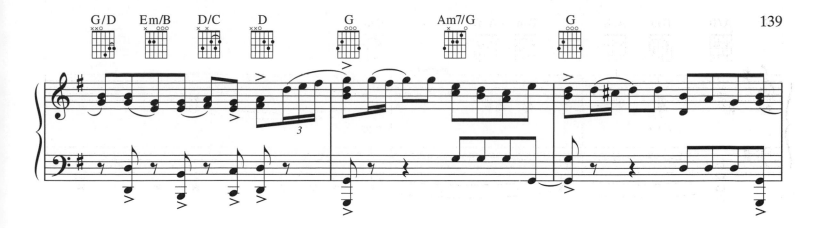

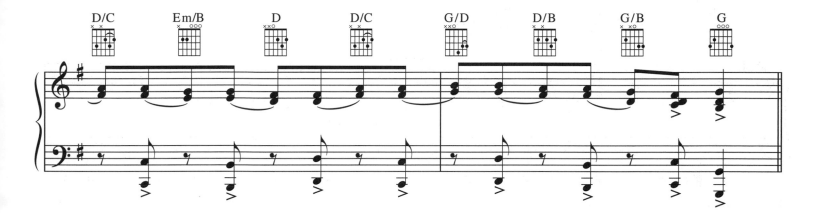

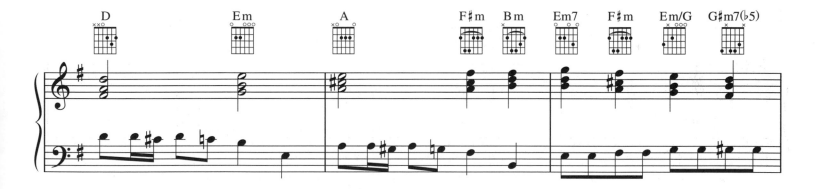

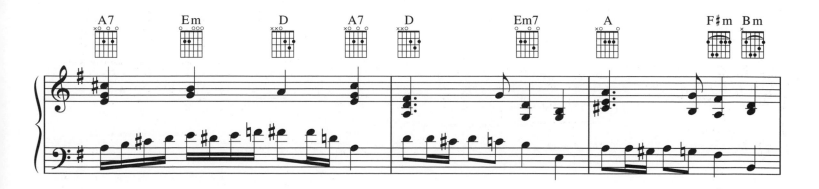

A Mad Russian's Christmas - 9 - 7

140

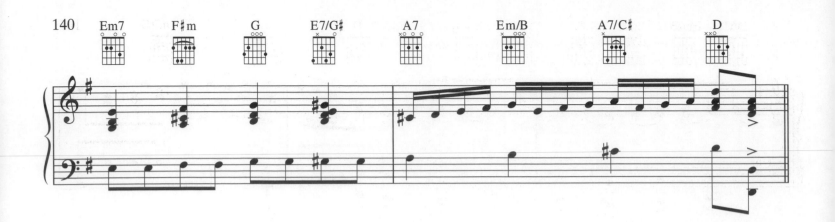

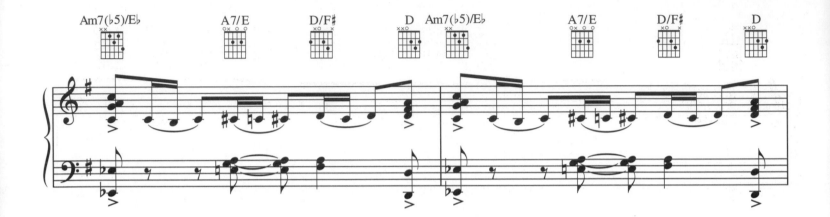

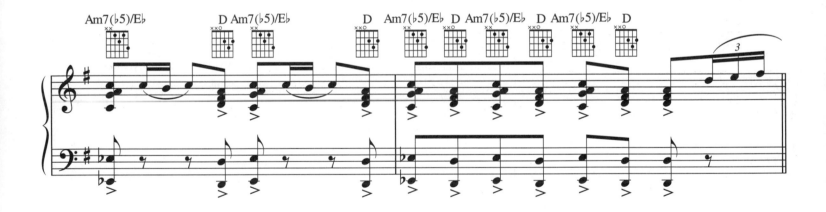

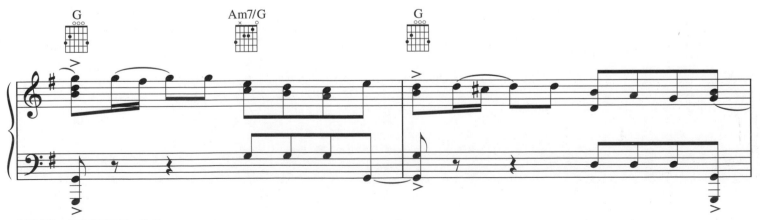

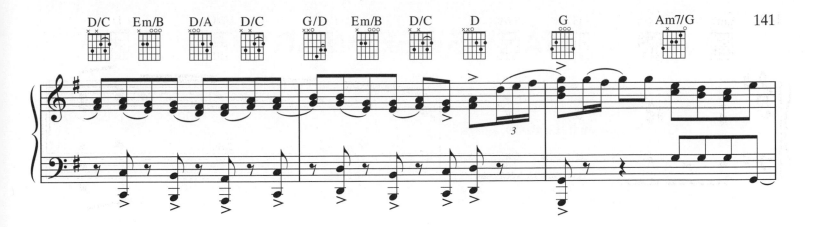

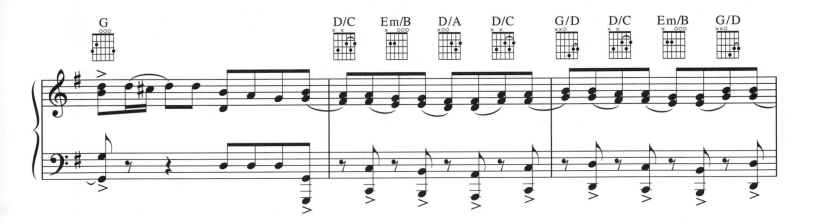

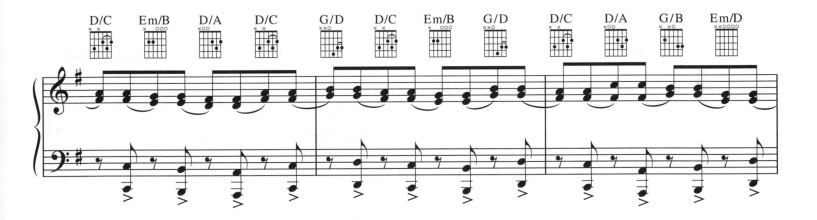

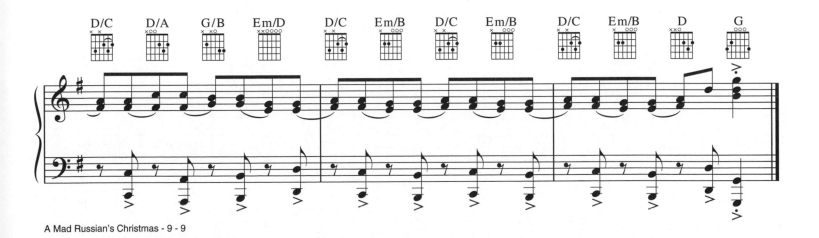

MARY SWEET MARY

Words and Music by
TIFFANY ARBUCKLE LEE
and KEITH THOMAS

Gently, somewhat rubato ♩ = 76

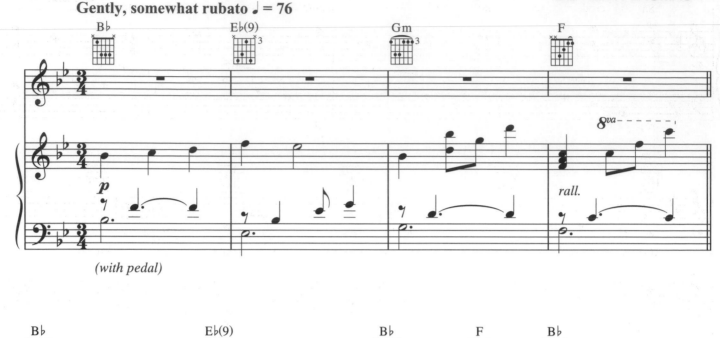

(with pedal)

Mar - y, sweet Mar - y, your heart o - ver - flows.

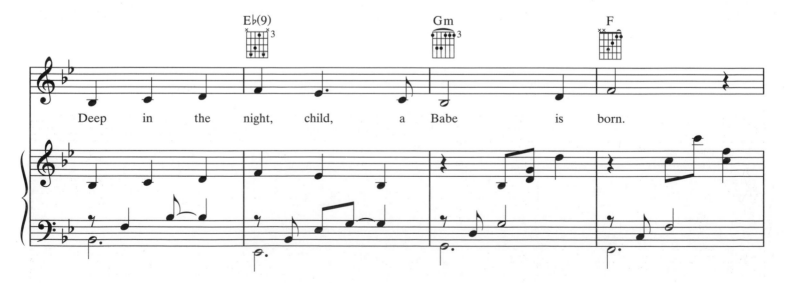

Deep in the night, child, a Babe is born.

144

Mary, Sweet Mary - 5 - 3

145

Mar - y, sweet Mar - y, God's pre - cious Child,

bless - ed re - demp - tion is found in His eyes.

Mary, Sweet Mary - 5 - 4

NUT ROCKER

By KIM FOWLEY

Nut Rocker - 3 - 1

148

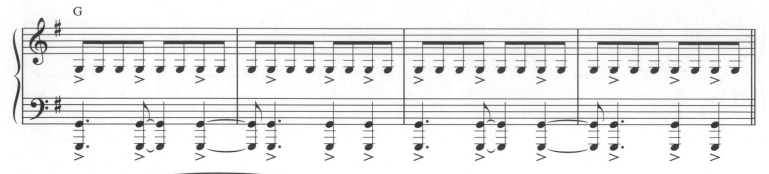

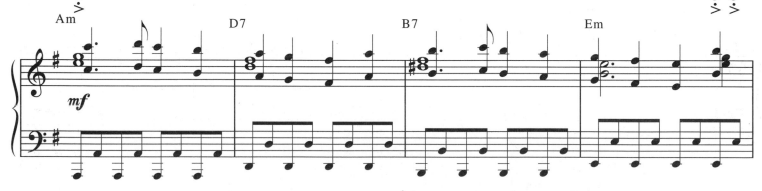

Nut Rocker - 3 - 2

G

Nut Rocker - 3 - 3

O COME, O COME, EMMANUEL

TRADITIONAL

O Come, O Come, Emmanuel - 2 - 1

O HOLY NIGHT

By ADOLPHE CHARLES ADAM
Arranged by JIM BRICKMAN

Moderately slow, with expression ♩ = 66

(with pedal)

O Holy Night - 4 - 1

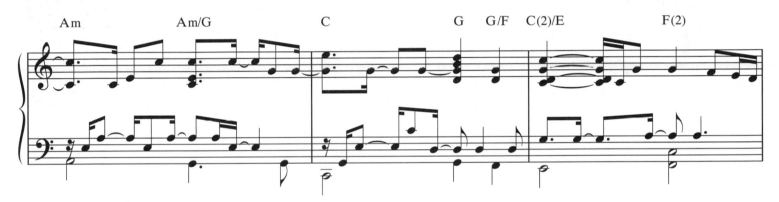

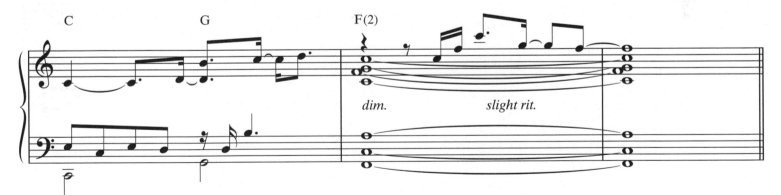

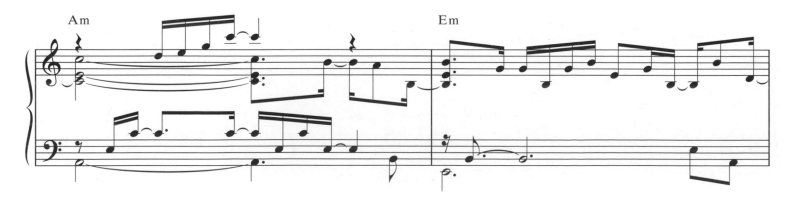

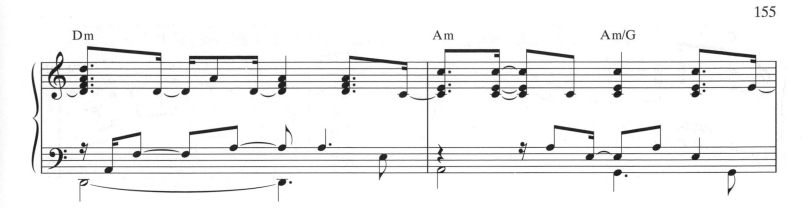

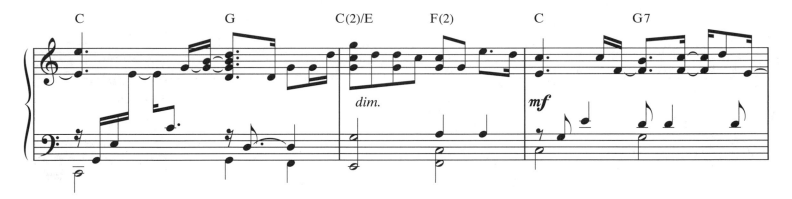

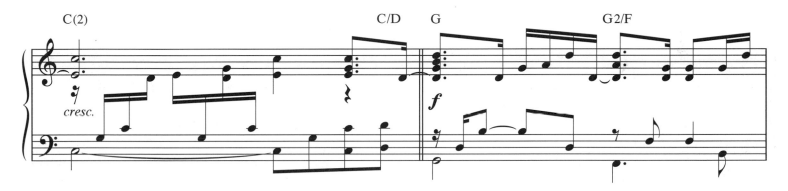

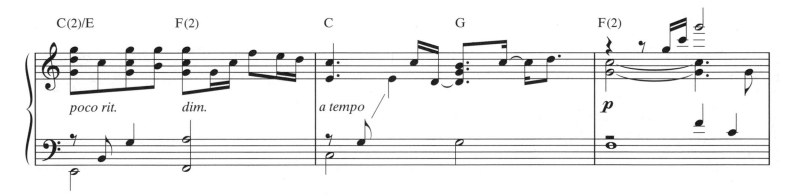

O Holy Night - 4 - 4

ROCKIN' AROUND THE CHRISTMAS TREE

Words and Music by
JOHNNY MARKS

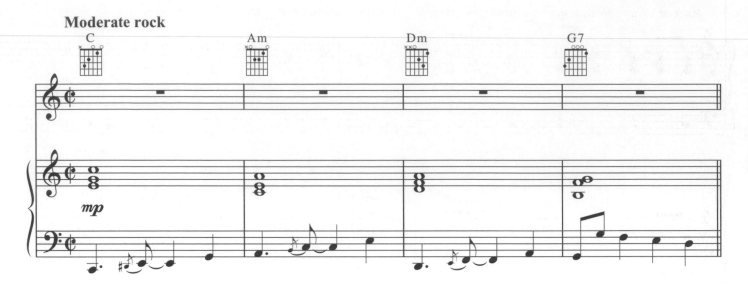

Rock-in' a-round the Christ-mas tree____ at the Christ-mas par-ty hop.____

Mis-tle-toe hung where you can see,____ ev-'ry cou-ple tries to stop.

Rockin' Around the Christmas Tree - 3 - 1

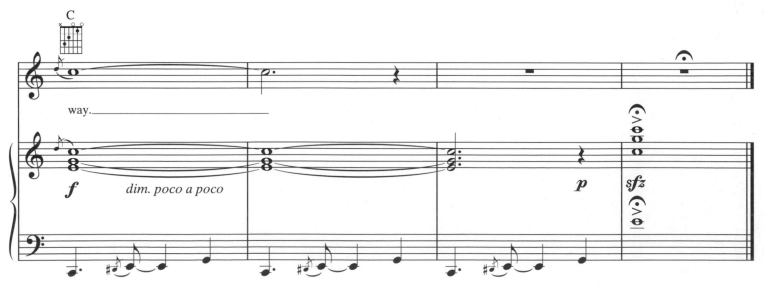

RUDOLPH, THE RED-NOSED REINDEER

Words and Music by
JOHNNY MARKS

Rudolph, the Red-Nosed Reindeer - 3 - 1

SANTA CLAUS IS COMIN' TO TOWN

Words by
HAVEN GILLESPIE

Music by
J. FRED COOTS

(alternate lyric) Now

just came back from a love-ly trip a-long the Milk-y Way.
San-ta is a bus-y man, he has no time to play.

Santa Claus Is Coming to Town - 6 - 1

I stopped off at the North Pole to spend a hol - i - day;
He's got mil - lions of stock - ings to fill on Christ - mas Day;
I
you'd

called on dear old San - ta Claus to see what I could see. He
bet - ter write your let - ter now and mail it right a - way, be -

took me to his work - shop and told his plans to me.
cause he's get - ting read - y, and his rein - deers and his sleigh.
So, you

Delicately
Refrain:

bet - ter watch out, you bet - ter not cry. Bet - ter not pout, I'm tell - ing you why:

mf

SILVER AND GOLD

Words and Music by
JOHNNY MARKS

Slowly and expressively

(with pedal)

Sil - ver and gold, sil - ver and gold,

ev - 'ry-one wish - es for sil - ver and gold. How do you

mea - sure its worth?_____ Just by the plea - sure it

Silver and Gold - 2 - 1

Silver and Gold - 2 - 2

SLEIGH RIDE

Words by
MITCHELL PARISH

Music by
LEROY ANDERSON

Moderately bright

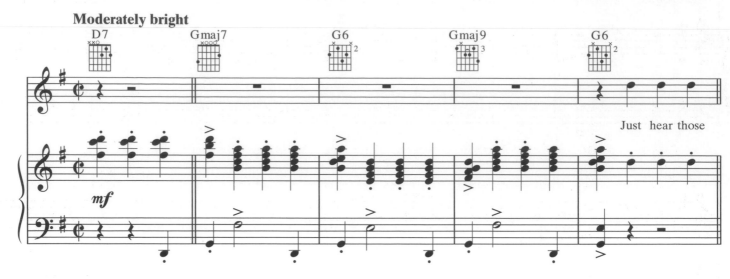

Just hear those

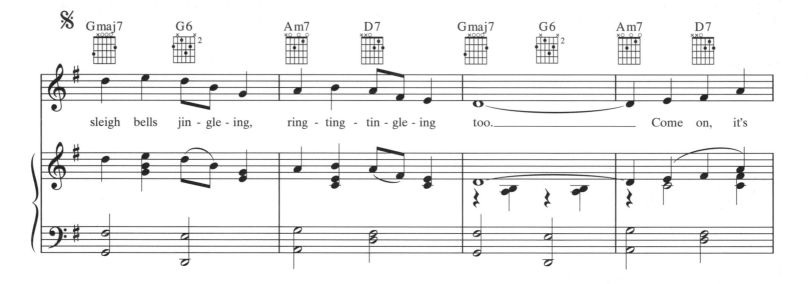

sleigh bells jin-gle-ing, ring-ting-tin-gle-ing too.____ Come on, it's

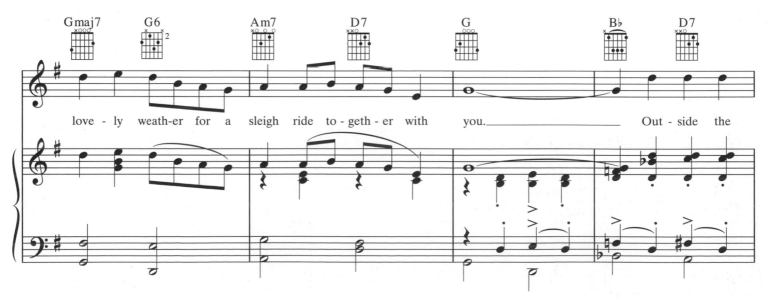

love-ly weath-er for a sleigh ride to-geth-er with you._____ Out-side the

Sleigh Ride - 6 - 1

snow is fall-ing and friends are call-ing, "Yoo hoo." _____ Come on, it's

love-ly weath-er for a sleigh ride to-geth-er with you. _____ Gid-dy-

yap, gid-dy-yap, gid-dy-yap, let's go, let's look at the show,

we're rid-ing in a won-der-land of snow. _____ Gid-dy-

172

Sleigh Ride - 6 - 3

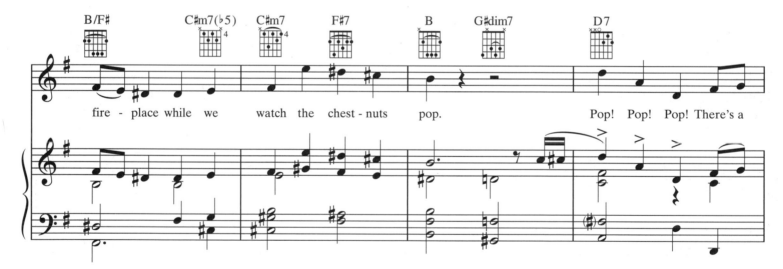

SNOW MISER

(from *The Year Without a Santa Claus*)

Words and Music by
JULES BASS and MAURY LAWS

Ragtime feel, with a light shuffle ♩ = 92

Refrain:

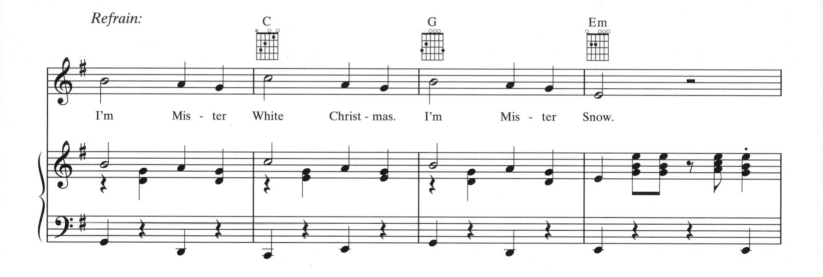

I'm Mis-ter White Christ-mas. I'm Mis-ter Snow.

I'm Mis-ter I-ci-cle. I'm Mis-ter Ten Be-low.

Snow Miser - 4 - 1

Friends call me Snow Mi - ser. What - ev - er I touch

turns to snow___ in my clutch. I'm too

much!

Refrain:

He's Mis - ter White Christ - mas. He's Mis - ter Snow.

UKRAINIAN BELL CAROL

Traditional

Ukrainian Bell Carol - 2 - 1

WE WISH YOU A MERRY CHRISTMAS

TRADITIONAL ENGLISH FOLK SONG

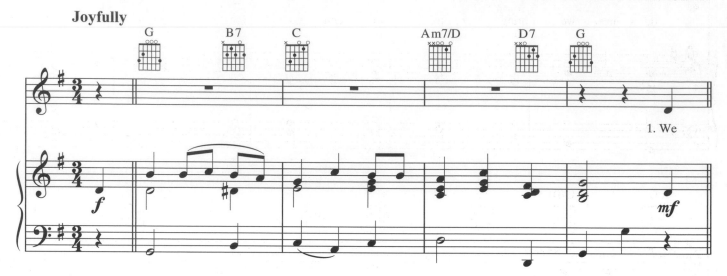

1. We

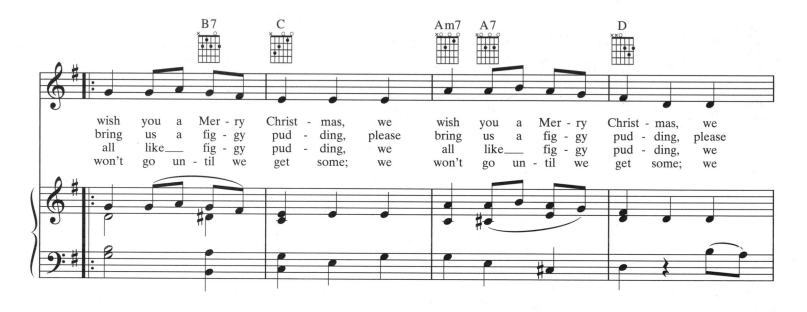

wish you a Mer - ry Christ - mas, we wish you a Mer - ry Christ - mas, we
bring us a fig - gy pud - ding, please bring us a fig - gy pud - ding, please
all like__ fig - gy pud - ding, we all like__ fig - gy pud - ding, we
won't go un - til we get some; we won't go un - til we get some; we

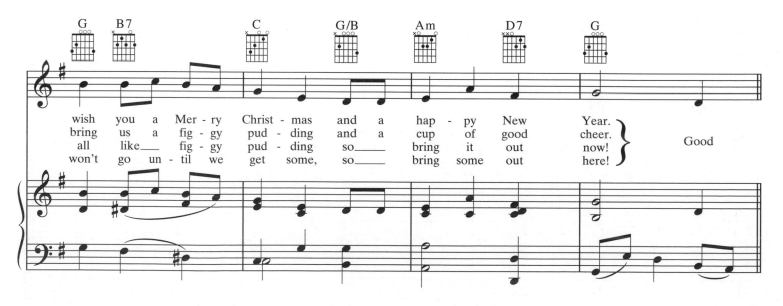

wish you a Mer - ry Christ - mas and a hap - py New Year.
bring us a fig - gy pud - ding and a cup of good cheer.
all like__ fig - gy pud - ding so__ bring it out now!
won't go un - til we get some, so__ bring some out here!

Good

183

We Wish You a Merry Christmas - 2 - 2

WHAT CHILD IS THIS?

Traditional
Arrangement by JIM BRICKMAN

Moderately slow, freely and flowing (♩. = 48)

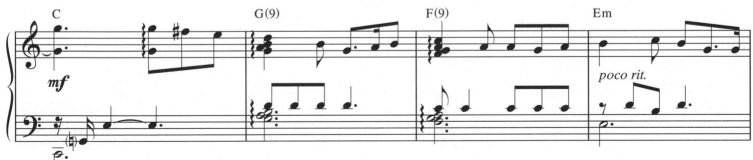

What Child Is This? - 4 - 2

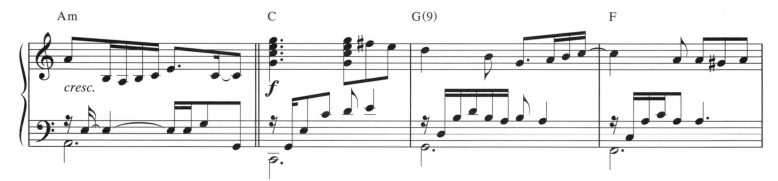

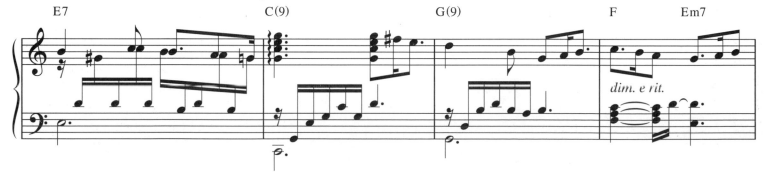

(♩ = 72)

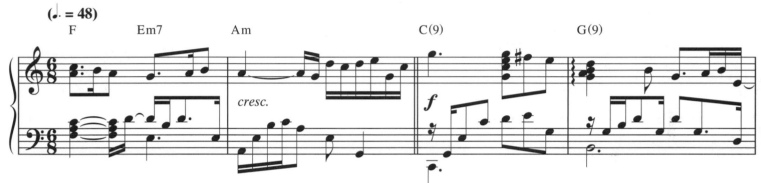

What Child Is This? - 4 - 4

WINTER WONDERLAND

Words by
DICK SMITH

Music by
FELIX BERNARD

WIZARDS IN WINTER

(Instrumental)

Music by
PAUL O'NEILL and ROBERT KINKEL

Moderately fast ♩ = 144

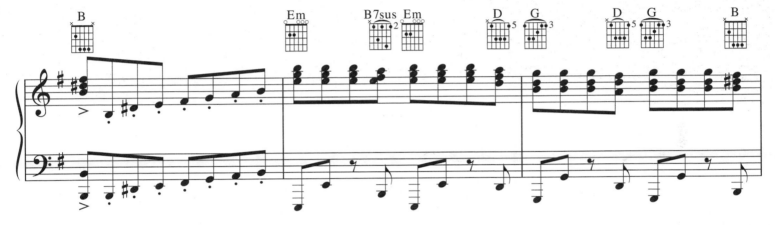

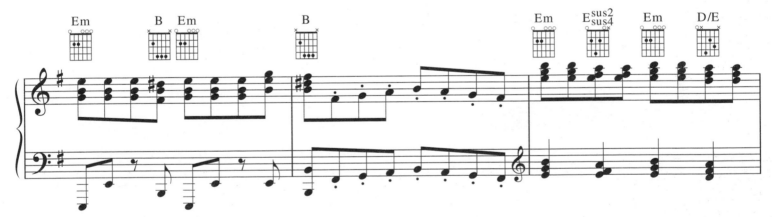

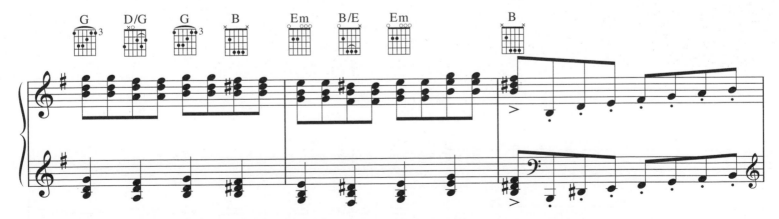

Wizards in Winter - 7 - 1

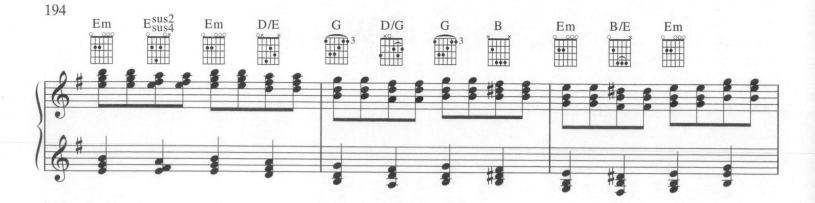

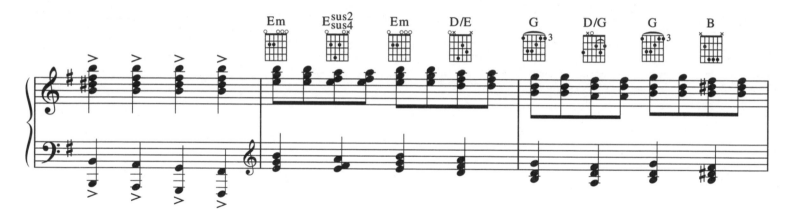

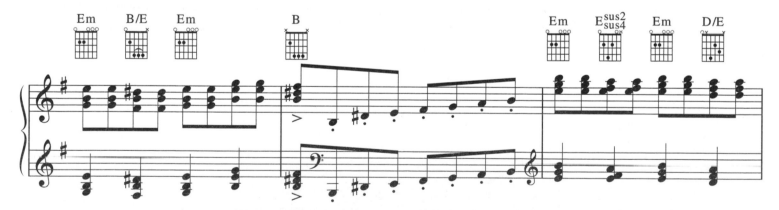

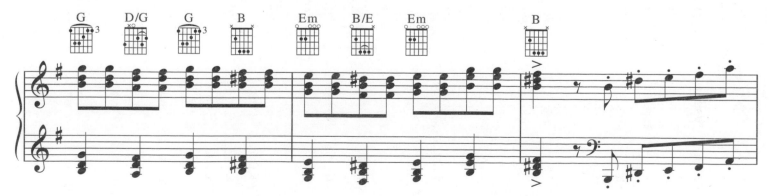

196

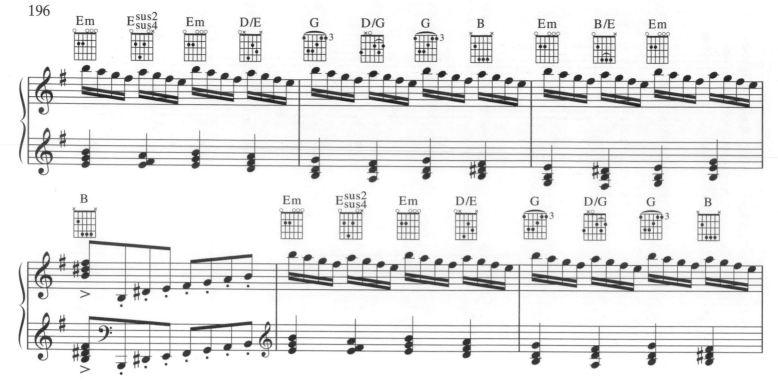

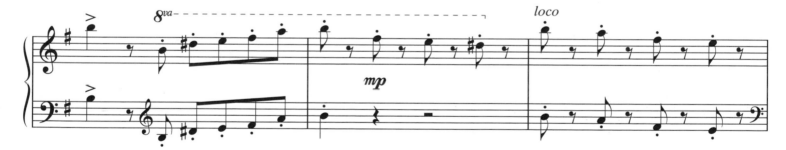

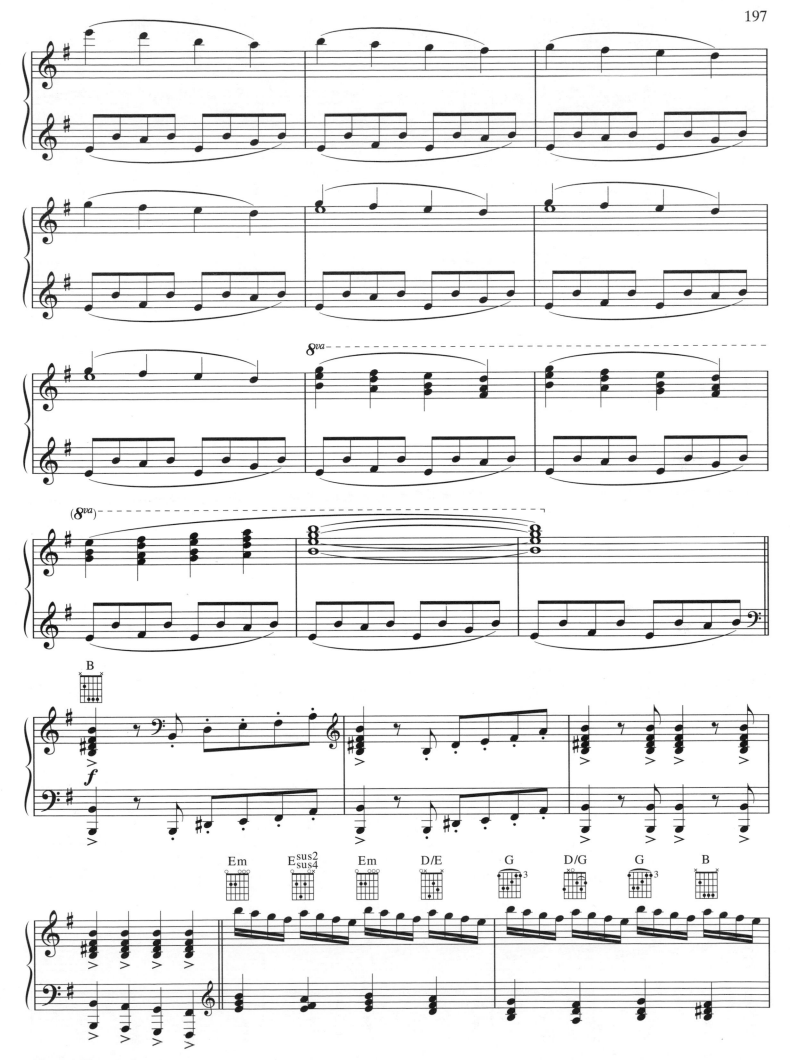

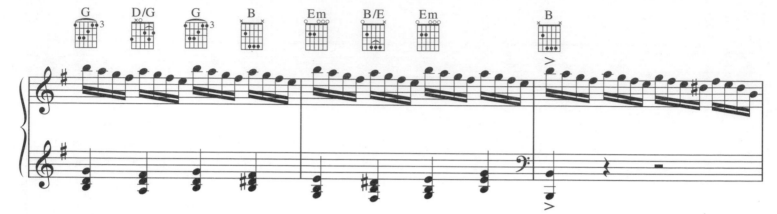

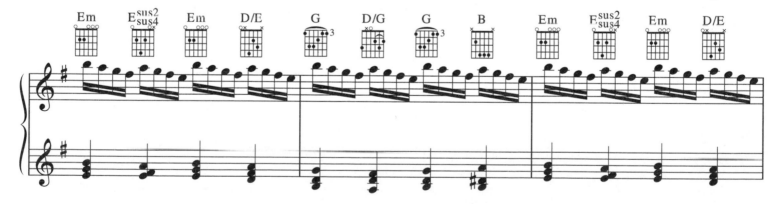

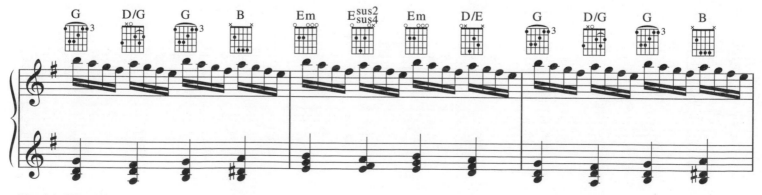

199

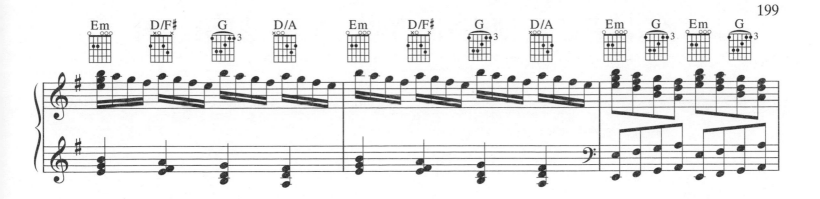

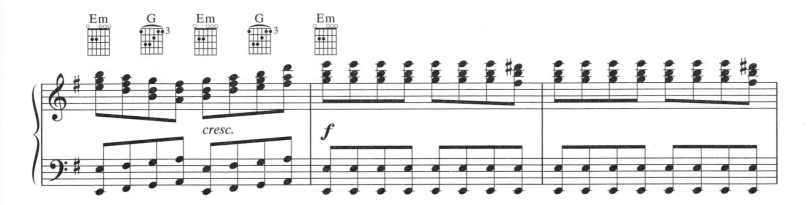

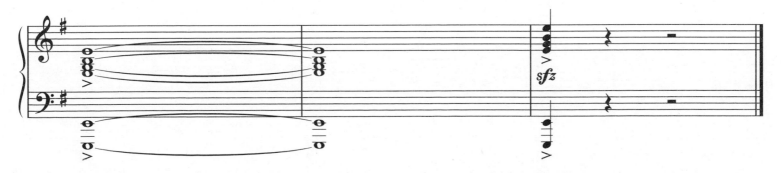

Wizards in Winter - 7 - 7

YOU'RE A MEAN ONE, MR. GRINCH

(from *How the Grinch Stole Christmas*)

Lyrics by
DR. SEUSS

Music by
ALBERT HAGUE

1. You're a mean one, Mis-ter Grinch! You___
2.–6. *See additional lyrics*

real-ly are a heel.___ You're as cud-dly as a cac-tus, you're as

You're a Mean One, Mr. Grinch - 2 - 1

Bb7 Ebmaj7 Ab7 D7(b9)

charm - ing as an eel, Mis - ter Grinch!_____ You're a bad ba - nan - a with a

1.2.3.4.5.
G7sus G7 Fm G7

greas - y black peel. 2. You're a

6.
G7sus G7 Cm

with ar - se - nic sauce!_____

ff

Verse 2:
You're a monster, Mr. Grinch!
Your heart's an empty hole.
Your brain is full of spiders,
You've got garlic in your soul, Mr. Grinch!
I wouldn't touch you with a
Thirty-nine-and-one-half-foot pole.

Verse 3:
You're a foul one, Mr. Grinch!
You're a nasty-wasty skunk!
Your heart is full of unwashed socks,
Your soul is full of gunk, Mr. Grinch!
The three words that best describe you
Are as follows and I quote:
Stink! - Stank! - Stunk!

Verse 4:
You're a vile one, Mr. Grinch!
You have termites in your smile.
You have all the tender sweetness
Of a seasick crocodile, Mr. Grinch!
(Spoken:) And given the choice between the two of you
I'd take the seasick crocodile.

Verse 5:
You're a rotter, Mr. Grinch!
You're the king of sinful sots.
Your heart's a dead tomato
Spotched with moldy, purple spots, Mr. Grinch...
(Spoken:) Your soul is an appalling dumpheap
overflowing with the most disgraceful assortment of
deplorable rubbish imaginable, mangled up in
...Tangled-up knots.

Verse 6:
You nauseate me, Mr. Grinch!
With a nauseous, super naus.
You're a crooked jerkey jockey
And you drive a crooked hoss, Mr. Grinch!
(Spoken:) You're a three-decker Sauerkraut
and toadstool sandwich
...with arsenic sauce.

You're a Mean One, Mr. Grinch - 2 - 2

SILENT NIGHT

Words and Music by
JOSEPH MOHR and
FRANZ GRUBER

1. Si - lent night, ho - ly night, all is calm,
2. Si - lent night, ho - ly night, shep - herds quake
3. Si - lent night, ho - ly night, Son of God,

all is bright, 'round yon vir - gin moth - er and Child. Ho - ly In - fant, so
at the sight. Glo - ries stream_ from heav - en a - far, heav'n - ly hosts_ sing,
love's pure light. Ra - diant beams_ from Thy ho - ly face, with the dawn of re -

ten - der and mild, sleep in heav - en - ly peace,___ sleep_ in heav - en - ly peace. birth.
"Al - le - lu - ia." Christ the Sav - ior is born.___ Christ_ the Sav - ior is born.
deem - ing grace, Je - sus, Lord, at Thy birth,___ Je - sus, Lord, at Thy